Giving Voice to
Critical Campus Issues

ACPA Media Board

Giving Voice to Critical Campus Issues

Qualitative Research in Student Affairs

Editor
Kathleen Manning

Contributors
Kelly Haggerty Ahuna, Jennifer Hart,
Melissa Regan, Elizabeth A. Skeffington,
Tim Wilson, and Michael Paul Wong

American College Personnel Association

Copyright © 1999 by
The American College Personnel Associations

University Press of America,® Inc.
4720 Boston Way
Lanham, Maryland 20706

12 Hid's Copse Rd.
Cumnor Hill, Oxford OX2 9JJ

Library of Congress Cataloging-in-Publication Data

Giving voice to critical campus issues : qualitative research in
student affairs / editor, Kathleen Manning ; contributors, Kelly
Haggerty Ahuna...(et al.).
p.   cm.
Includes bibliographical references.
1. College students—United States—Case studies. 2. College
students—Research—United States. 3. Universities and colleges—
United States—Sociological aspects—Case studies. I. Manning,
Kathleen. II. Ahuna, Kelly Haggerty.
LA229.G548   1999   378.1'98—dc21   98-32256 CIP

ISBN 1-883485-13-4 (cloth: alk. ppr.)
ISBN 1-883485-14-2 (pbk: alk. ppr.)

⊖™ The paper used in this publication meets the minimum
requirements of American National Standard for Information
Sciences—Permanence of Paper for Printed Library Materials,
ANSI Z39.48—1984

To
Egon Guba
who opened the door to qualitative research
to me and countless others

Contents

Introduction

Kathleen Manning

Being a professor in higher education means that I am often witness to students' extraordinary efforts. The research projects summarized in this book were conducted as part of a qualitative research class that I taught at the University of Vermont. These projects were conducted over a period of years and several classes. The chapter authors, now student affairs professionals, were graduate students in the Higher Education and Student Affairs masters program at the University of Vermont.

In the qualitative research class we explored a different way of thinking from traditional scientific methods. The emphasis was on "emergent paradigm thinking": subjectivity is accepted and encouraged over objectivity; multiple realities are mined; interpretations are privileged over generalizations; and values are explored and taken into account during the research process.

This book highlights the central place of constructivist research in higher education. By making meaning of qualitative data (i.e., words), the authors expose the richness of university life. This understanding is essential to high quality administrative practice.

The primary purpose of this book is to construct understandings of complex issues on college campuses. The people whose perspectives are represented in the case studies are those whose views are rarely fully explored in research reports. The voices enacted are a university custodian, residence life staff member, resident assistant, adult child of an alcoholic, and undergraduate students. The people involved in the research are not the power brokers or "movers and shakers" of an institution. They are the staff and students who work behind the scenes to keep the campus community intact. They play an essential role in university life. The case studies reveal the silences that are as much a part of campus life as faculty senates, public meetings, and policy making.

I want to thank the students and respondents for sharing their work with a wider higher education audience. They most likely do not consider themselves researchers, so sharing these studies is an act of courage. Their generosity and efforts indicate what we, as educators are capable of.

1

Setting the Context

Kathleen Manning

No one can tell the one, eternally true, perfect story about the way the world is; but we can tell some stories about ourselves, nature, and social life which can be shown with good evidence to be far less partial and distorted—less false—than the dominant ones. (Harding, 1991, p. 60)

College campuses are communities filled with people of diverse talents, varied means to express their joys, and unique perspectives that guide their lives. These positive aspects of campus life are accompanied by the reality that these community members also carry burdens. The research in this book gives voice to the perspectives of people who have experienced these matters first hand. A rich discernment of these issues and the people affected by them can lead to higher quality student affairs administration.

The research reported in this book relies on a methodology, constructivist inquiry, which allows the participants (i.e., respondents) to fully express their voices and perspectives. The data collection and analyses seek to obtain an in depth understanding about people and the context in which they live and work. Through detailed methodological procedures, the researcher and respondents are closely connected, collaborate about the research findings, and act as co-researchers. Constructivist researchers explore the topic under study to achieve as close an understanding of the respondents' experience as possible. This understanding is then conveyed through case studies, documentary films, and other products of the research process.

Purposes of the Collection

The primary purpose of this book is to construct understandings of complex issues of concern on college campuses. This aim is achieved through the presentation of case studies concerning suicide, acquaintance rape, alcohol-related student death, classism, adult children of alcoholics, and multiracial identity.

Unifying Themes

Several themes unify the collection of case studies: identity; the complexity of campus life; links to considerations beyond oneself; complexity, distinctiveness, and dynamism; and expression of unheard, unacknowledged voices.

Identity

The research summarized in the chapter case studies expands the enduring theme of college student identity. Specifically, several aspects of this concept are explored: (a) identification of one's existential life purpose in reaction to a peer's death (Chapters 3 and 5); (b) gender identity in relation to pressures concerning sex, power, and gender dynamics (Chapter 4); (c) integrity and personal ethics as conceived through one's work (Chapter 6); (d) independence and the "gift of self" formed within, as well as in opposition to, one's family of origin (Chapter 7); and (e) multiracial identity in a society which dictates monoraciality (Chapter 8). These themes concerning identity add to the understanding of existing identity development theory, among them works by Baxter Magolda (1992), Belenky, Clinchy, Goldberger, and Tarule (1986); Chickering and Reisser (1993), Cross (1991); Gilligan, (1982); and Sue and Sue (1990).

Complexity of College Life

Student development theorists conceived their theories, including identity development, within campus climates dissimilar from today's environment. While the 1960s, the first decade of student development theory, included social ferment and intense self-exploration, the critical issues explored here (suicide, acquaintance rape, alcohol-related student death, classism, adult children of alcoholics, and multiracial identity) are more obviously present on today's campus than in the 1960s.

Significant changes have occurred in American society over the last 30 years including decreased reliance on social institutions such as houses of worship, increased single parent households, and political ferment about civil rights issues. These changes add to the complexity of college campuses which have also experienced significant changes: rising costs, diverse populations, increased accountability, and decreased public confidence. Current students, regardless of age, arrive on campus with more potent issues than previous generations. Understandably, pressure on student affairs educators to intervene in critical campus issues has increased.

Link to Consideration Beyond Oneself

The respondents are committed to considerations which extend beyond individual self-interest. Many, if not all, spoke of a dedication to their institution; and a need to connect themselves to people and objects beyond individual self-interest. Each participant has a sense of self that takes community into account. The case studies illustrate the theme that campus involvement, personally and professionally, counts for something in the lives of these community members.

Complexity, Distinctiveness, and Dynamism

A third theme within the case studies is the knowledge and meaning to be gained by student affairs faculty, students, and practitioners who use constructivist inquiry. Constructivist inquiry is a method of qualitative research which emphasizes meaning, multiple perspectives, and the dynamism of human experience. An overarching purpose of constructivist inquiry is to comprehend the complexity of every day, human existence. This purpose is in direct contrast to traditional, quantitative research in which generalizations are discovered then applied to populations for the purpose of prediction and control. Where similarity of experiences and behavior is studied in quantitative research, differences and distinctiveness are emphasized in constructivist inquiry. Where stability and similarity across contexts are assumed in quantitative research, dissimilarity and dynamism even within similar contexts are assumed in constructivist research. These themes of complexity, distinctiveness, and dynamism are vividly portrayed in the case studies.

Chapter 2 briefly summarizes the methods of constructivist research and places it in a student affairs context. Hence, this book can be used by faculty members in student affairs graduate preparation programs, qualitative research classes, and residence life, peer counseling, and orientation undergraduate education classes. Practitioners can gain a vicarious experience by reading the case studies, expand their perspectives on campus life, and gain understandings which can inform their practice.

Unheard, Unacknowledged Voices

An essential aspect of constructivist inquiry is its capacity to dig deeply into a topic, explore overlooked voices, and tease out varied points of view. In keeping with this tradition, the respondents whose words are represented in this book are not college presidents (Bensimon & Neumann, 1993; Birnbaum, 1992), faculty members undergoing socialization (Whitt, 1991); campus cultures as seen from an administrative perspective (Tierney, 1988), or administrative leaders on college campuses (Amey & Twombly, 1993). While those topics are important, this book takes a different approach.

The respondents portrayed here are an undergraduate suicide survivor, resident assistants, a custodian, an adult child of an alcoholic, and an undergraduate multiracial student. The purpose of this book is to create a space where the respondents' meaning can be expressed within the cacophony of campus voices.

By examining college life through the lenses of the students, staff, and para-professional staff, student affairs educators can gain insights about their roles, experiences, and meaning-making processes. Readers can view their practice and campus life through lenses (e.g., women, people of color, and under represented university members) different from their own. As such, these perspectives can be considered during policy making, decision making, programming, staff selection, and other administrative practices. Residence life staff, new professionals, faculty members, and others can vicariously experience the issues provided in the case studies before encountering those incidents in the field.

The authors do not pretend that these cases take the place of direct experience; but the insights offered can provide an opportunity to raise questions. What could be done in the event of a student suicide? What identity struggles might an adult child of an alcoholic have?

What are the feelings I might experience when one of my residents dies? Reading the case studies gives administrators and students the opportunity to consider their responses and conceivable actions before the crisis occurs.

Criteria for Case Study Selection

The topics for these cases were selected by the chapter authors as part of a graduate-level course, "Qualitative Research in Higher Education," at the University of Vermont. The case studies are final and culminating assignments from that class. Impressively and unapologetically, these case studies are the authors' first research efforts. The excellence of the case studies speaks to the talent of these researchers as well as the fact that high quality, meaningful research which says something important can be conducted by people at varying levels of research expertise. The cases were selected by the editor for inclusion in this book on the following criteria:

a. Sound methodological procedures,

b. Vivid and evocative portrayal of the respondents and topic,

c. Ability to convey the central concerns of a vital campus issue,

d. Rich portrayal of the complexity of campus life, and

e. Relevance to student affairs practice.

Within the case studies there was an effort by the authors to generate discussion about the topics at hand. Each author raises questions, provokes a response, and asks the reader to come to a deeper understanding and interpretation of administrative practice. The authors challenge readers to fashion conclusions about students, campus life, and the challenging situations in which educators find themselves. The cases are emotional and sometimes disturbing. They seek to displace any myths about the safety and comfort of campus life. Without being prescriptive or heavy handed, the authors are instructive.

But the instructive nature of the case studies should not be taken as guidelines for what *all* people who fit the respondents' characteristics think and feel. The reader is cautioned not to approach this research seeking indisputable answers about suicide, acquaintance rape, alcohol, class, and multiraciality. The insights and implications in this book point to opportunities for informed, inclusive student affairs practice, not generalizations across groups of diverse students.

The Collection

The first case, "The Griefwork of Suicide Survivors," written by Kelly Ahuna, provides a stirring account of a resident assistant who experienced a resident's suicide. Ahuna presents the respondent's words through the case study in an evocative first-person voice. This form clearly conveys the respondents' emotions and the co-constructed nature of the research Ahuna conducted. During the data collection process, the respondent sought to make sense of her emotional experience in relation to her personal and professional life.

Ahuna's work provides information for residence life staff as they struggle to understand student suicides. This intent is furthered by the implications for practice offered. Questions raised through the case study include, what are some of the emotions raised for residence life staff during a student crisis? What information and training should be provided to staff prior to experiencing a student suicide? How can staff help others? What does residence staff need to do to help themselves in the event of a student suicide? This case study, in particular, can be skillfully used as a source for discussion during resident assistant and professional staff training.

Chapter 4 contains the case study, "The Languages of Acquaintance Rape," written by Melissa Regan. Through the case she explores two voices, one female and one male, as they discuss campus acquaintance rape. Using the respondents' words, the author gives the reader a first hand picture of the social life of undergraduate students. The case study is presented in a comparison format to illustrate the voices, impressions, and opinions of the two respondents. In Chapter 4, Regan incorporates theory into her data to form a synthesis of theory and original constructivist research. As in Ahuna's chapter, implications for administrative practice and policy considerations are offered as concluding remarks. This chapter can be used in programming for undergraduate students. One can role play the different genders to make the voices come to life for students. Through this enactment, the respondents' words can be a source of insight and discussion during presentations and workshops.

Chapter 5, "Picking Up the Pieces: A Case Study of the Death of a Resident," was written by Elizabeth Skeffington. Another first-person account, this case study vividly describes the emotional aftermath of a resident assistant who experienced the alcohol-related death of a floor resident. The case relates his grief, feelings about his resident assistant role, and view of the devastating effects of alcohol on students. One can appreciate how this resident assistant coped in a crisis and withstood the emotional toll taken on him. This case study can be folded into resident assistant training activities as an illustration of crisis management. What is more important, through use of this case in training, resident assistants can begin to comprehend the unfathomable thought that they could experience such a tragedy.

"Respect and Dignity in the Free Marketplace of Ideas: Working Class Resistance within the University" was written by Michael Paul Wong and is contained in Chapter 6. This case represents the experience of a female custodian who understands the university through a well-developed set of ethics and standards for practice. As one with access to the upper-level administrative offices on campus, this respondent has a unique perspective on the decision and policy making that abounds in such a setting. Wong adroitly leads us through the darkened hallways of his respondent's nightly routine to present a unique and often overlooked perspective on campus life. Wong's research findings can be used in student affairs graduate preparation programs as a case study to explore the ethical considerations of all campus community members.

Chapter 7 contains "Footsteps of Courage: A Case Study of Felice" a case study written by Jennifer Hart. Hart, similar to Ahuna and others, wrote in the first-person style to portray an undergraduate student who is an adult child of an alcoholic (ACOA). The respondent's experiences of growing up with an alcoholic father and the courage with which she faces these circumstances are demonstrated in this chapter.

Hart's case contrasts with the student development theories that present identity development as a consecutive, stage-like process. While not the case with all development theory, there is often a normatively defined process regardless of students' individual attributes or backgrounds. While student affairs educators fully understand that students pursue their development in unique ways, the theory often aggregates groups of students (e.g., African American students, women, first-year students) for ease of explanation. Hart's chapter explores the nuances of identity development by delineating the differences for an ACOA student. This portrayal can be used in educational and training efforts with peer educators, counselors, and others.

The final case study, Chapter 8, was written by Tim Wilson and is titled, "You Know I'm Triracial, Right?" The evocative case introduces us to Res, a triracial undergraduate student. In a world which asks Res to "check only one box," Wilson helps student affairs educators and others understand the dynamics of being multiracial. Another first-person account, the case can assist college administrators and faculty to see that racial identity is a fluid, socially constructed phenomenon.

Case Study Style and Format

These cases, though nonfiction and based on specific data collection and analysis procedures, read like novels. As clear portrayals, they give profound and in depth depictions of individuals, events, or points of view (Lightfoot, 1993). This depth, a strength of constructivist research, is also a disadvantage. The cases illustrate only a narrow sliver of campus life—depth not breadth.

The reader should know that the first-person case studies were carefully constructed from the respondents' words, with full permission and understanding of the style. In all instances, the implications of appropriating a respondent's voice when using the first-person were thoroughly discussed by the researchers and respondents. If the respondents disagreed with the use of the first-person voice, the authors suggested an alternative style.

All case studies, first-person and otherwise, were carefully member checked by the respondents (see Chapter 2) to assure that words, feelings, and experiences conveyed as the respondent's were perspectives that she or he actually discussed. If the respondent was uncomfortable with any manner in which she or he was portrayed in the case, the language of the case study was changed. This method, briefly introduced in Chapter 2 and demonstrated in the subsequent chapters, can be further explored through an examination of the sources listed in the reference sections.

References

Amey, M., & Twombly, S. B. (1993). Re-visioning leadership in community colleges. In C. Conrad, A. Neumann, J. Haworth, & P. Scott, *Qualitative research in higher education: experiencing alternative perspectives and approaches* (pp. 527–544). Needham Heights, MA: Ginn Press.

Baxter Magolda, M. (1992). *Knowing and reasoning in college: Gender-related patterns in students' intellectual patterns.* San Francisco, CA: Jossey-Bass.

Belenky, M., Clinchy, B., Golberger, N., & Tarule, J. (1986). *Women's ways of knowing: The development of self, voice, and mind.* New York, NY: Basic Books.

Bensimon, E. M., & Neumann, A. (1993). *Redesigning collegiate leadership: Teams and teamwork in higher education.* Baltimore, MD: Johns Hopkins Press.

Birnbaum, R. (1992). *How academic leadership works: Understanding success and failure in the college presidency.* San Francisco, CA: Jossey-Bass.

Chickering, A., & Reisser, L. (1993). (2nd ed.). *Education and identity.* San Francisco, CA: Jossey-Bass.

Cross, W. (1991). *Shades of black: Diversity in African-American identity.* Philadelphia, PA: Temple University Press.

Gilligan, C. (1982). *In a different voice: Psychological theory and women's development.* Cambridge, MA: Harvard University Press.

Harding, S. (1991). *Whose science? Whose knowledge?: Thinking from women's lives.* Ithaca, NY: Cornell University Press.

Lightfoot, S. (1993). Afterword: The passion of portraiture. In C. Conrad, A. Neumann, J. Haworth, & P. Scott, *Qualitative research in higher education: Experiencing alternative perspectives and approaches.* (pp. 397–404). Needham Heights, MA: Ginn Press.

Sue, D. W., & Sue, D. (1990). *Counseling the cultural different: Theory and practice.* Wiley & Sons.

Tierney, W. (1988). Organizational culture in higher education: Defining the essentials. *Journal of Higher Education, 59,* (1), 2–21.

Whitt, E. (1991). "Hit the ground running": Experiences of new faculty in a School of Education. *Review of Higher Education, 14,* (2), 177–197.

2

Conducting
Constructivist Inquiry

Kathleen Manning

Student affairs professionals have struggled since the field's inception
to understand the complexities of student development and growth.
In this search for knowledge, qualitative research, a method emphasizing depth of understanding over breadth, has been central to
the formation of student affairs theory. Arthur Chickering (1969) used
data from interviews with Goddard College students to construct his
developmental vectors. Carol Gilligan (1982) used qualitative analysis to generate insights about women's psychological development. Marcia Baxter Magolda (1992) in her longitudinal study on epis-
temological stages used inductive reasoning, a qualitative research
method.

The method used for the studies in this book is constructivist
inquiry, formulated by Yvonna Lincoln and Egon Guba (1985; Guba
& Lincoln, 1989). Constructivist inquiry emphasizes the multiple perspectives of respondents, ethical obligations of the researcher to her
or his respondents, and techniques required to meet standards of quality. Similar to many qualitative research methodologies, constructivist
inquiry relies on interviewing, observation, and document analysis as
a means of data collection. Data analysis is conducted through an

inductive process of culling patterns and themes from the data rather than fitting the data, through deductive reasoning, into categories determined in advance.

This chapter explains the basics of constructivist research so that the reader can understand the studies reported here. Regrettably, only a brief explanation of the method is possible in this limited space. I hope to whet the reader's appetite for the wealth of information about qualitative research. Topics included in this chapter are purposes of constructivist research, paradigm considerations, methodological procedures, and quality and rigor.

Purposes of Constructivist Research

The purpose of constructivist inquiry is to produce depth of understanding about a particular topic or experience. This research differs from conventional quantitative research which defines average or normative behavior, makes generalizations about how all or most people act, and offers common characteristics shared across groups. Qualitative researchers seek *verstehen* or the "profound insight and comprehension of something's/one's essence" (Lincoln, 1988, p. 61). Holistic understanding, meaning-making, and interpretation are essential concerns in qualitative research (Patton, 1990). These methods can generate powerful insights about the complex issues students face in college.

Constructivist inquiry is well-suited to knowledge discovery about campus life. Through an open and trusting relationship between researcher and respondent, a "slice of life" or perspective is shared. These perspectives, expressed in a descriptive and interpretive written account (e.g., case study), are conveyed in all their emotional and personal distinction. The case, if it evokes emotions from the reader, can render a vicarious experience impossible through statistical and quantitative analysis.

Through the meaning communicated in the case studies, campus life can be better understood, college policy decisions more capably fashioned, and administrative decision-making skillfully achieved. The knowledge gained through qualitative research is as rich and complex as the lives upon whom the findings are based. The researcher is successful when she or he untangles the web of complexity that characterizes the respondents' lives and guides the reader to *verstehen*.

Focus of the Studies

Each study reported in this book was bounded by a research focus, purpose, or question determined prior to data collection. Although foci often changed as data are collected, the foci for the enclosed studies are:

1. To draw connections between griefwork and the experience of a suicide survivor;

2. To explore the languages of male and female respondents as they discussed rape;

3. To better understand alcohol-related tragedies and the experiences of residence life staff;

4. To examine, through research conducted with a female university custodian, how one can make meaning of the contradictions and congruencies between the fundamental ideals of equality and liberty and the reality of work in a class-based society;

5. To inform educators about the experience of an adult daughter of an alcoholic, with a particular emphasis on identity development;

6. To determine how a triracial person develops his racial identity in a monoracial setting.

These foci were sharpened as the individual designs unfolded. In several circumstances, the respondents provided the most useful insights about the purpose and uses of the research.

Paradigm Considerations

Constructivist inquiry differs from quantitative research at the level of beliefs or assumptions; the emergent paradigm underscores this method. Assumptions include the idea that truth is not objective but rather socially constructed from the experiences, background, perceptions, and thought processes of humans. The researcher's task is to work diligently to understand the multiple realities of the respondents, research context, and others who influence the information being shared. Since research is generally conducted in communities, the task of sorting through, understanding, and conveying the multiple realities among respondents is one of the most difficult and interesting tasks of constructivist inquiry. The emergent paradigm is represented in physics by theory after Einstein (e.g., relativity, quantum physics), popular films such as "Jurassic Park," and popular business literature such as Peters and Waterman's (1982) *In Search of Excellence.*

Emergent Paradigm Assumptions

The assumptions of the emergent paradigm (Guba, 1985; Guba & Lincoln, 1989; Lincoln & Guba, 1985; Reason & Rowan, 1981) include the following:

1. The researcher and respondent have a close, subjective, collaborative relationship;

2. The research products are not generalizable to all or most circumstances but, rather, interpretable only within local contexts. Insight, meaning, and understanding, rather than broad application, are the goals of the research;

3. Rather than a singular Truth which holds reliably in all cases, multiple truths are socially constructed, time- and history-bound. Most important, there are many truths depending on the points of view of those involved in the research;

4. The methodology cannot escape, nor does it try to escape, the values of those involved: researcher, research setting, methodology, underlying theory, and respondents.

These emergent paradigm assumptions are expressed in the research projects summarized in this book in several ways:

Trust

Trust was carefully built and scrupulously maintained between the researchers and respondents. The respondents were not simply means to acquire data. Data were obtained from respondents in a process emphasizing respect, collaboration, and reciprocity.

Co-constructed Interpretations

In keeping with the trust built through the data collection phase, the researchers did not single-handedly analyze the data, compile the findings, and write the case study. The researchers worked with their respondents to co-construct the interpretations, determine the information to be presented in the case studies, and choose a case study format in concert with the respondents' style. As such, the task of writing each case study, while the responsibility of the researcher, was guided by the respondent.

Value Driven

Traditional science, using the conventional paradigm (e.g., singular truth, objective relationship between researcher and respondents, value neutrality, and generalization as the ultimate goal) (Guba & Lincoln, 1989), assumes that the researcher's values and perspectives (i.e., biases) must be isolated and eliminated. The qualitative research tradition represented here makes no such claim. Values are understood always to affect research and can be used as lenses through which to interpret the data. To ignore the values of the researcher, respondents, or research setting means to overlook major sources of influence and insight: the perspectives through which people construct and view their realities and truths.

Researcher Assumptions

Since it is taken as a given that values will affect the study, an essential aspect of constructivist inquiry is an examination of the researcher's assumptions. The researcher scrutinizes her or his expectations, feelings about the topic under study, and fears and joys concerning the study. The goal of this effort is for the researcher to understand the lenses through which she or he constructs the study's focus, asks interview questions, and chooses the data depicted in the case study. This process of clarifying the researcher's taken for granted assumptions is significantly facilitated by peer debriefing (see High Quality and Rigor section) wherein peers discuss methodology issues, including assumptions "hidden" from the researcher.

While a complete explanation of the emergent paradigm is not the purpose of this book, a review of its assumptions can aid readers to understand the research tradition used in the studies presented here. Additional information about emergent paradigm research can be obtained in resources listed in the reference section of this chapter.

Methodological Procedures

The following sections describe the general procedures used to conduct the studies reported in this book. Any variations from the approach outlined in this chapter are discussed in the methodology sections of the individual chapters.

Entry and Access to Respondents

Student affairs staff have unique advantages when it comes to gaining access and entry to respondents. Their significant interactions with students, accessibility to various campus offices, and exposure to a broad array of campus life expands their range of choices for research topics and respondents.

Entering a research site and identifying respondents are among the most difficult tasks of qualitative research. While people generally enjoy talking about themselves once contact is made, identifying respondents who are knowledgeable about the topic under study, have sufficient time, and are available through all stages of the research process can be frustrating and fraught with false starts and dead ends.

Entry and access negotiations are not completed when contact is made with the respondent, but take place throughout the research. The focus of the study, consent, and boundary negotiations are explained each time a new respondent is recruited for the study. Attention to the political nature of research and the discomfort that people have about "being studied" are to be heeded. After permission or consent to conduct the study is received from campus authorities, the characteristics necessary to build an adequate sample are determined.

Purposive Sampling

Purposive sampling was originated by Patton (1990) as a strategy by which one could learn or come to understand a particular subject. Unlike random sampling where representativeness for the purpose of generalizing is the goal, the researcher uses purposive sampling to identify people with particular characteristics. The researcher uses criteria to locate respondents who are likely to be knowledgeable about the topic being studied. Patton suggested four categories to guide respondent selection:

(1) sampling extreme or deviant cases, (2) sampling typical cases, (3) sampling for maximum variation (picking three or four cases that

represent a range on some dimension), (4) sampling critical cases, and (5) sampling politically important or sensitive cases (Lincoln, 1985, p. 146).

The emphasis for the enclosed studies centered on choosing respondents who were exemplar representatives of the topic under study. In other words, the respondents chosen included people who had done a significant amount of thinking about the focus of the study. They were people who could articulately express their distinctive experiences. While reticent respondents are not actively avoided in constructivist inquiry, data collected from respondents who enjoy talking about their experiences and points of view is richer and more extensive than data generated from shy, restrained interviewees.

The unethical practice of dual roles (e.g., friend and respondent; employee and respondent) was avoided by the researchers. They contacted respondents who were knowledgeable about the study's focus yet unknown to themselves. Gatekeepers were employed as "go betweens"—persons who serve as points of entry for the researchers (Bogdan & Biklen, 1992). The gatekeeper often made the first contact with the respondent so that the potential interviewee did not feel obligated or unduly pressured to participate in the study. The use of gatekeepers is especially important in research topics which are sensitive and could result in a breach of confidentiality (e.g., rape survival).

Responsibilities to the Respondents

Respondents were apprised of the time commitment being asked of them, degree to which confidentiality could be assured, and requirements of the methodology. Respondents were assured that the data, at all stages of the studies, belonged to them. If at any point the respondent changed her or his mind about participation in the study, she or he was free to cut off contact with the researcher. At this time the researcher was obligated to return all field notes and data. This commitment was reinforced through a consent form, signed by the researcher and respondent, outlining the parameters of the mutually agreed upon arrangement. In many cases, the researcher and respondent negotiated the consent form in a manner which set the tone for the collaborative and co-constructed nature of the research.

Data collection is not a primary concern during access, entry, and respondent identification. Realistically, however, data are collected from the first point of contact with potential respondents until the final parting.

Data Collection

The research summarized in this volume is based on data collection with one or two respondents. Not typical of constructivist or qualitative research, the purpose of this narrow range of respondents was to closely focus the data collection and meaning derived from data analysis. As the instructor of the qualitative research class in which these studies were undertaken, I felt that it would be unethical to ask students to undertake research with a wide, expansive scope. A completed, well-done study with a clearly defined focus is a more productive and preferable contribution to the student affairs field than an incomplete, broadly defined research project. Readers should note that sampling, particularly the appropriate number of respondents, is a highly contested issue in qualitative research. A sufficient number of respondents depends on the focus of the study, depth of data to be collected, and individual characteristics of the research context.

Data collection methods in constructivist research include interviewing (i.e., one-on-one conversations between the researcher and respondent), observation (e.g., meetings, student activities, class presentations), and document analysis (e.g., memos, college yearbooks, student journals, e-mail messages). Interviewing and observation were the predominant methods used in the studies in this book.

Interviews

Multiple interviews were held with the respondents until patterns and themes repeated. When this point of redundancy was reached, the researcher knew that the data collection was nearing an end. Trust was established during the interviewing by asking the respondents to choose the interview site. The emphasis was on the respondents' comfort, not the researchers' convenience.

The research foci were maintained by following Lincoln and Guba's (1985) advice of treating each interview as a "guided conversation" (Guba, 1985). While initially open ended, the guided conversations were not invitations for respondents to discuss anything that came to mind. Questions based on the foci were generated by the researchers in advance of the interviews. Many times, these questions were not explicitly asked because the respondents judged the information about the topic which was most important to share. Gentle prompting and competent listening skills often serve the researcher better than a formal interview protocol. But questions generated in advance of the interview assist the researcher when respondents are unsure of the research focus or need prodding to stay on topic.

Observation

In several cases, data were collected by observing the respondent in a particular situation (e.g., classroom, student activity). Skeffington observed her respondent in a class where his alcohol-related death experience became the inspiration for an art project. Wong observed and interviewed his respondent as she conducted her late night custodial responsibilities.

Document Analysis

While document analysis was not used in the studies contained here, the literate culture of higher education generates a rich array of written materials. Letters to home by students, memoranda documenting the evolution of a policy, and electronic mail archives are all sources of written documents. These can be collected and analyzed in the same manner as interview and observation data. The data generated from document analysis are a source of categories, themes, and interpretations.

Data Recording

Data, including direct quotations and respondent observer comments, were noted in a field journal (e.g., steno or legal pad) used during the interview or observation. The data from the field journal were then transcribed and expanded as field notes, usually via a computer. Some researchers, for example Regan with her research concerning acquaintance rape, recorded the respondents and transcribed the interviews verbatim from the audio tape recordings. Regardless of the method used (e.g., transcription or re-constructed notes from memory and the field journal), the field notes became the raw data of the analysis process.

Human as Instrument

The instrument or means of data collection in qualitative research is the human being or researcher. Different from quantitative paper and pencil surveys or instruments, the human as instrument is able to sense feelings, probe promising areas, and closely observe the nuances of human communication. As discussed earlier, the researcher uses his or her lens and personal perspective as a means through which to view the data. As such, she or he needs to be fully aware of how these lenses might distort as well as illuminate what is seen and heard. At all times, the researcher remains cognizant of the fact that the respondent, not the researcher, is the central focus of the research. A researcher with an ax to grind or point to make will over-represent her or himself in the findings and under-represent the respondents. Safeguards against these tendencies (e.g., peer debriefing, prolonged engagement, persistent observation) are discussed below (see High Quality and Rigor).

Data Analysis

Inductive Reasoning

Inductive reasoning begins with the data as a source of interpretation or explanation. This analysis contrasts with the investigative style of deductive reasoning where data verify and/or support hypotheses posited in advance. In other words, in quantitative research, the theory is proposed, data are collected, and the analysis of the data verifies or disproves the theory. In constructivist inquiry, data are collected prior to any theorizing. These data are then inductively analyzed into categories, expanded into themes, and folded into interpretations and findings. The resultant inductively generated interpretations are called grounded theory (Strauss & Corbin, 1990). A method used to generate grounded theory, constant comparative analysis (Glaser & Strauss, 1967), is described below.

Constant Comparative Analysis

In constant comparative analysis, the researcher separates the field notes into discrete, stand-alone ideas or units which are then printed onto index cards. These cards are sorted into categories based on their similarities and differences. The researcher postpones naming the categories, but instead lets the inductive process of similarity and difference determine what data fit what groupings. These categories are then added to, adapted, and expanded as subsequent data collection activities are conducted. When the categories are saturated (i.e., additional information does not add meaning to the emerging themes), the data collection is complete. These categories become the backbone upon which to build the research interpretations and findings.

Although the inductive process of constant comparative analysis was used by the researchers in these studies, each went about the process in a different way. Wong used Hyperqual, a software package, to build the analysis and interpretation of his data. Hart and other researchers used the tried and true "cut and paste" method of physically dividing the data, printing it on index cards, and categorizing it manually (Lincoln & Guba, 1985). In all cases, the researchers combed the data for themes and categories from which they could build their interpretations.

Skillful analysis occurs when the researcher digs deeply into the data, examines underlying assumptions to ferret out meaning, and places the respondents' experiences into a fuller context of human living. This analysis becomes the source inspiration for interpretations which are then expressed through the case studies.

Data analysis is one of the most difficult steps in constructivist inquiry. A significant amount of insight, soul searching, and creativity is needed to generate findings which are conceptually rich, descriptively vivid, and analytically fruitful. Most of us can, with some effort, write a good story. But the purpose of constructivist inquiry is to collaborate with the respondents to write a case study which provides insight for practitioners, meaning for readers, and vision for educators.

Writing the Research Report

Qualitative research findings are often presented in case studies although documentary films, research reports, and other means are also used. During the writing of the case study, significant data analysis occurs. The researcher chooses the data to be presented in the case, makes interpretations of the data in conjunction with the respondents, and writes the case study as an interpretive text (Geertz, 1973). The case study is more than description; it is a conceptually and analytically rich piece of writing.

The case study form accommodates the grounded theory in the form of themes, interpretations, and working hypotheses providing a narrative account of the findings. Case studies can be organized in a variety of ways: thematically, question and answer, realist tale, first-person account, and researcher as narrator, among other forms.

Expressing the Voices of the Respondents

Respondents' and researchers' voices are expressed in case studies through a collaborative effort based on care, trust, and genuineness. These qualities are achieved through careful methodological procedures (e.g., authenticity) closely adhering to ethical practice (e.g., "do no harm").

A pressing issue regarding this collaborative effort is the presentation of the respondents' and researcher's voices. Substantial literature has been written about the privileges inherent in the researcher's position. When one has university titles and degrees, money with which to conduct the research, and confidentiality requirements directing that the respondents' names be withheld, the issue of who *really* owns the data becomes an issue.

Regardless of the choices made, the issues of authorship and voice remain contested:

> Ethical problems emerge in framing a case study. . . . how much of the researcher's "self" should be introduced into the case report? To what extent does the researcher speak with an "authorial voice," taking the role of the "professional stranger"? To what extent may the researcher be "informed and transformed" in the process? (Lincoln & Guba, 1989, p. 234).

While I and the chapter authors do not pretend to have solved the ethical dilemmas concerning authorship, we assure the readers that we collaborated with the respondents to avoid, as much as possible, the appropriation of their voices and experiences. This collaboration included thorough member checking, negotiated use of consent forms which outlined the rights of the respondents, and peer debriefing. In the end, while these issues can never be completely resolved, conversations with respondents and significant soul searching resulted in a satisfactory though still conflicted resolution about the location of the researcher's voice in the case study.

First-Person Voice

The cases presented in Chapters 3, 5, 7 and 8 by Ahuna, Skeffington, Hart, and Wilson are written in first-person format. The reader should note that these cases were written by the chapter authors, not the respondents. Because they did not want to fall into the trap of appropriating another's voice and words, the authors worked closely with the respondents to communicate the implications of using the first-person format. To do so, the researchers exercised careful member checking throughout the research process. Findings and interpretations were carefully co-constructed with the respondents whose voices are so personally represented. These steps are essential if the first-person voice is to be invoked in a case study.

The first-person voice and case study format work well with topics that are personal, emotional, and stirring. The reader should be warned that the first-person account is not the only or the predominant means of reporting qualitative data.

In addition to the first-person format, other case study styles are represented in this volume. Wong, for example, places himself squarely in the case study as the researcher. As the narrator and visitor to the respondent's place of work, Wong makes no effort to hide his presence. The conversations he had with the respondent during data collection are clearly evident in the case study. The voices of the respondents in Regan's study ring true as their words are placed, verbatim, into the case study. As she juxtaposes the respondents' words about acquaintance rape, one can hear the voices in her modified question and answer format case study.

High Quality and Rigor

High quality findings are a goal of constructivist inquiry. To that end, several techniques are recommended to constructivist researchers.

Consent Forms

Upon entry to the sites and respondents, each researcher negotiated informed consent. This process is a requirement of all human subjects research as well as an ethical consideration in constructivist inquiry. The form used to solidify consent assured the respondent that confidentiality would be maintained through the use of a pseudonym; he or she would be involved in decisions about data use; the data belonged to him or her and could be withdrawn at any point; and any aspect negotiated by researchers and respondents would be treated seriously. Furthermore, permission was obtained from the respondents for use of the research in both the course and this book.

The consent form was handled with extreme care in these research projects. Negotiated during the first contact with potential respondents, the manner in which the consent form was presented and negotiated set the tone for subsequent meetings. If the respondent felt that he or she was being "studied" without reciprocity or respect, that negative tone would have persisted throughout the research.

Member Checking

Member checking is the

process of continuous, informal testing of information by soliciting reactions of respondents to the investigator's reconstruction . . . and to the constructions offered by other respondents or sources. (Lincoln & Guba, 1986, p. 77)

All field notes, patterns and themes gleaned from the data, summaries of interpretations, and drafts of case studies are checked by respondents for accuracy, clarification, and assurance that the findings generated are congruent with their perspectives (Manning, 1997).

Member checking is conducted to assure that the research findings emerge from, and remain true to, the respondent's experience. In keeping with the trusting, collaborative nature of constructivist inquiry, the respondents must be involved in each step of the process. While this means of assuring quality is often omitted in qualitative research, it is essential to the authenticity of any study (Lincoln & Guba, 1986; Manning, 1997). If the researcher does not stay close to and attuned with the respondents' meaning through member checking, data become distant from and irrelevant to their experiences.

Methodological Journal

Researchers are advised to use a methodological journal as a medium to explore their feelings, note methodological decisions, explore interview questions, and examine issues needing comment (Ely, Anzul, Friedman, Garner, & Steinmetz, 1991; Lincoln & Guba, 1989). The information in this journal is often written into the methodological section of research reports. Combined with peer debriefing (see below), the methodological journal can be a link to sanity and support during an often times lonely research process.

Peer Debriefing

Each researcher was involved in a peer debriefing group for the duration of his or her project. This group was composed of fellow researchers who offered support, methodological checks, and insights about the projects. While the peer debriefing groups were initially given questions to consider (e.g., what's the focus of your study? how will you locate respondents? what are the themes emerging from your study?), these groups evolved in ways unique to the researchers' needs. The psychological and emotional support afforded within peer debriefing groups is invaluable.

An essential task of peer debriefing groups is to check the researcher's unacknowledged assumptions. As colleagues who have been with the researcher since the inception of the project, peer debriefers often recognize when themes are inductively generated from the data or when they reflect the researcher's perspectives with no accompanying corroboration in the data.

Prolonged Engagement

The researcher achieves prolonged engagement, and adds breadth to the study, by staying in the field sufficiently long enough to fully understand the context, issues at hand, and perspectives (Lincoln & Guba, 1986). In the case studies in this book, the short time frame of the studies is a concern. While the data collection and analysis were conducted over a limited period of time (e.g., four months), the researchers and I do not view this circumstance as a threat to the usefulness of the studies. Other measures of quality and rigor (e.g., member checking, co-construction and collaboration with respondents, member checking, and persistent observation) were met and add to the quality of the research.

Persistent Observation

The researcher is involved in the "lengthy and intensive contact with the phenomena (or respondents) in the field to . . . identify saliences in the situation" (Lincoln & Guba, 1986, p. 77). A researcher must stay engaged in the research site in such a way that he or she understands the important aspects of the respondents' lives and context. Adding depth, persistent observation permits the researcher to focus the research effort in a way that eliminates scattered and obscure data.

These techniques are only several of those available to assure rigor and quality in constructivist inquiry. A fuller discussion of authenticity and attendant techniques is available in Manning (1997).

Conclusion

This chapter provides a brief overview of constructivist inquiry for the purpose of apprising the reader of the methods used in these studies. Because a complete explanation of the methodology cannot be achieved in such a short space, the reader is encouraged to explore further the kind of research represented in this book.

In reading the following chapters, student affairs professionals and other educators are encouraged to consider the following questions:

1. What insights, gleaned from the cases, can be folded into your knowledge base?

2. What practices, policies, and programs can be recommended as a result of the vicarious experience acquired through your reading of the case studies?

3. How can these cases be used during professional and student staff training as examples of the crises they may experience in their work with students?

4. What institutional structures can be implemented for students, staff, and faculty in an effort to be proactive about the issues discussed in this book?

While qualitative methodology does not allow broad generalizations across all students or staff, the cases in this book can provide significant insights for policy making, program planning, program evaluation, and administrative practice. We hope you will find the results and recommendations as compelling as we did throughout the research process.

References

Baxter Magolda, M. (1992). *Knowing and reasoning in college: Gender-related patterns in students' intellectual development.* San Francisco, CA: Jossey-Bass.

Chickering, A. (1969). *Education and identity.* San Francisco, CA: Jossey-Bass.

Ely, M. with Anzul, M., Friedman, T., Garner, D., & Steinmetz, A. M. (1991). *Doing qualitative research: Circles within circles.* New York, NY: Falmer Press.

Geertz, C. (1973). *The interpretation of cultures.* New York, NY: Basic Books.

Gilligan, C. (1982). *In a different voice: Psychological theory and women's development.* Cambridge, MA: Harvard University Press.

Glaser, B., & Strauss, A. (1967). *The discovery of grounded theory: Strategies for qualitative research.* Chicago, IL: Aldine.

Guba, E. (1985). *The context of emergent paradigm research.* In Y. Lincoln (Ed.). Organizational theory and inquiry: The paradigm revolution. (79-104). Beverly Hills, CA: Sage.

Guba, E., & Lincoln, Y. (1989). *Fourth generation evaluation.* Beverly Hills, CA: Sage.

Lincoln, Y. (1985). The substance of the emergent paradigm: Implications for researchers. In Y. Lincoln (Ed.), *Organizational theory and inquiry: The paradigm revolution* (pp. 137–160). Beverly Hills, CA: Sage.

Lincoln, Y. (1988). "Naturalistic inquiry: Politics and implications for special education." Speech delivered for Project Directors' Meeting, Research in Education of the Handicapped.

Lincoln, Y., & Guba, E. (1985). *Naturalistic inquiry.* Beverly Hills, CA: Sage.

Lincoln, Y., & Guba, E. (1986). But is it rigorous? Trustworthiness and authenticity in naturalistic inquiry. In D. Williams (Ed.), *Naturalistic evaluation* (pp. 73–84). San Francisco, CA: Jossey-Bass.

Lincoln, Y., & Guba, E. (1989). Ethics: The failure of positivist science. *Review of Higher Education, 12,* 221–240.

Manning, K. (1997). Authenticity in constructivist inquiry: Methodological considerations without prescription. *Qualitative Inquiry, 3*(1), 93-115.

Patton, M. (2nd ed.) (1990). *Qualitative evaluation and research methods* (2nd ed.) Beverly Hills, CA: Sage.

Peters, T. J., & Waterman, R. H. (1982). *In search of excellence: Lessons from America's best-run companies.* New York, NY: Harper & Row Publishers.

Reason, P., & Rowan, J. (Ed.) (1981). *Human inquiry: A sourcebook of new paradigm research.* New York, NY: Wiley & Sons.

Strauss, A., & Corbin, J. (1990). *Basics of qualitative research: Grounded theory procedures and techniques.* Newbury Park, CA: Sage Publications.

3

The Griefwork of Suicide Survivors

Kelly Haggerty Ahuna

When a college student commits suicide, shock waves permeate the campus. Surviving students are faced, perhaps for the first time in their lives, with the process of grieving, and student affairs educators may be called upon to provide support and assistance to survivors. While student affairs educators face many challenges, they remain faithful to the original commitment of providing college students with out-of-classroom opportunities to learn, grow, be challenged and supported (American Council on Education, 1937). Thus, it is understandable that suicide "postvention," assistance in the healing process after a suicide, has become a student affairs responsibility.

As suicide statistics among college students rise, colleges and universities struggle to provide appropriate postvention for students affected by this form of student death. While existing research does not show how this is accomplished, there is a substantial amount of research on the process of grieving or "griefwork" that should be utilized to inform student affairs educators about bereavement as well as assist them in their work with surviving students.

This chapter draws connections between griefwork and the experiences of suicide survivors. A residence life staff member's perspective is presented through a case study which explores her experience, while an undergraduate, as a witness to a suicide. When the respondent's issues are compared to common themes in griefwork, t   h   e reader will see similarities, realize the uniqueness of each survivor's griefwork process, recognize possible effects of suicide on other students, and learn approaches to be utilized in preparing for suicide postvention.

Literature Review

Van Der Wal (1989) pointed out that although a significant amount has been written about suicide, very little research describes "the fate of those who have been left behind" (p. 149). It can be understandably difficult, therefore, for student affairs educators to accurately assess and successfully meet the needs of survivors.

Stephenson (1985) described grief as:

> an overwhelming and acute sense of loss and despair. The entire personality is helplessly engulfed in strong, sometimes frightening, feelings. The individual can feel out of control as monstrous waves of emotions sweep over him or her. Tossed about on this emotional sea, the familiar and secure landmarks of life are no longer in their usual places, the old meanings do not apply, and the individual may see him—or herself as the victim of forces outside of his or her control. (p. 121)

Stephenson, however, went further to identify differences in the kinds of grief people experience. He clarified that "only by understanding the meaning of the death to the griever can we come to understand the meaning of the grief" (p. 126). He therefore separated responses to death into two categories: reactive grief and existential grief. The void in life created by the loss of a loved one is indicative of reactive grief. In contrast, the realization of one's mortality and the subsequent inner turmoil resulting from a death is indicative of existential grief. When a member of the college community commits suicide, some survivors will feel the loss of a significant person in their lives. Many others, though, will be plagued with confusion, question their mortality, and re-evaluate the meaning of their lives.

Phases of Griefwork

Stephenson (1985) identified three phases in understanding grief: reaction, reorganization, and recovery. The reaction phase commonly includes feelings of numbness, bewilderment, and anger. Numbness, which allows survivors to continue everyday responsibilities and avoid strong feelings about the death, results in a delayed grief reaction. Bewilderment varies with the degree that the death was anticipated; a more sudden and unexpected death can result in severe reactions (LaGreca, 1988). Because there is usually no anticipation of a suicide victim's death, surprise is high, reaction is strong, and bewilderment prevails.

Anger, another common reaction in the first phase of grieving (Stephenson, 1985), is intensified with a suicide (Webb, 1986). "The intentional component of suicide foments rage in the survivors, who must confront the painful realization that the deceased renounced all possibility for help from them" (p. 470). People consider it unacceptable and disrespectful to be angry at the deceased and this is often transformed into guilt (Stephenson; Webb).

In the second phase of grief, disorganization and reorganization, survivors can intellectually continue an organized life, but existential grief shadows activities with doubt. The bereaved may feel that the world is incomplete and previous activities meaningless. The "former frame of reference" (Stephenson, 1985, p. 137) evaporates, and survivors struggle to reprioritize their lives. Moreover, a suicide can precipitate anxiety about survivors' impending deaths. This reminder fosters intense existential grief which is magnified if the survivor has no previous experience with grieving. The first encounter with death can be especially overwhelming and instigate a reaction similar to fear.

"Behavioral contagion," copying a particular behavior (e.g., suicide) after it is performed by a model, is a concern during the reorganization phase of grieving (Range, Goggin, & Steeded, 1988). A peer's suicide may reinforce suicidal thoughts and feelings of another and/or encourage that student to act on those feelings (i.e., suicide copying). Student affairs educators need to be cognizant of behavioral contagion as they meet the needs of surviving students.

The third and final phase of recovery described by Stephenson (1985) is reorientation and recovery. During this phase, survivors function easily in the external world, although the previous phases may have reorganized that world. Thoughts of the dead do not elicit intense grief reactions and earlier feelings of anger and guilt are resolved. The amount of time it takes survivors to reach this final stage varies widely. As student affairs educators react to a suicide, most of their work with survivors will focus on the initial two phases.

Methodology

The focus of this study, the griefwork of a college student after a successful suicide, was chosen because of my personal experience. In my first year in a residence hall staff position, a first-year resident committed suicide. As the hall advisor in the victim's building, I was intimately involved in the facilitation of recovery for the 180 residents. As a result of this professional and personal experience, I undertook a qualitative study of suicide in an attempt to inform readers of issues survivors face as they cope with such a tragedy.

I sought to create a document that could have assisted me as I struggled with my issues and those of others who looked to me for guidance. Likewise, I sought to conduct research which could inform other student affairs educators under similar circumstances. Rather than making generalizations, however, I leave the application of the teachings in the case study in the hands of the reader. Thick description in the case study clarifies the context in order to increase the possibility of maximum interpretation.

Respondent Identification

The research goal was to understand the healing process of suicide survivors and discover the intricacies of the griefwork of a student who had experienced a suicide. As I began purposive sampling, I met a student affairs professional who had, six years earlier, witnessed the suicide of a fellow resident when she was a sophomore at another university. She was an ideal respondent. Her vivid memory of and reactions to the suicide provided the student perspective I desired. The intervening years gave her significant time to construct meaning. Her position as a student affairs professional gave her another useful outlook on the situation. Because her professional role involved working with suicidal students or students reacting to a suicide, she could speak from another voice; the voice of the helper as well as the helpee. Therefore, the story and information I received from the respondent was more than sufficient to meet the goals of the research.

Case Study Format

When I undertook the case study composition, I was faced with the dilemma of choosing a writing style that would most effectively reach the reader and remain true to the respondent's voice. I decided to write the case study in the first person while incorporating my interpretations into the narrative, thus creating a truly co-constructed document. While I was tempted to make some dramatic and explicit statements of meaning and interpretation, those direct kinds of comments would not have been faithful to the respondent's voice. I resisted the urge to write too much of the researcher's voice in the case study. Instead, much of the case study is either directly quoted or closely paraphrased from the respondent's remarks and provided themes and interpretations for the reader in the context of the respondent's words. These themes were carefully member checked with her to ensure that they were a faithful portrayal of her experience with suicide.

Authenticity

The educative authenticity of this study became clear through the member checking process. The respondent had never related the story of the suicide in so much detail; she found value in her comprehensive rememberings and my questions. Likewise, my own value bound opinions of college suicide were stretched and refined. This study allowed me to outwardly focus my ideas and energy about suicide in a productive way.

Case Study

I can't believe that it's been six years already. Will this fall weather ever stop reminding me? What a really horrible, really awful day that was. Late October sophomore year of college. I remember it like it was yesterday. Coming home from my Thursday late night class, it was already 9:30 P.M. by the time I walked into my room. My roommate was home—as per usual at that time of night. I had no sooner taken off my coat and thrown my book-bag on the floor when I heard the noise. Jesus, what a noise that was—this huge, loud noise. I wonder if I'll ever stop hearing it. It sounded like a giant man had a handful of baseball bats and smashed them against a concrete wall as hard as he possibly could.

Our curtains were closed when I flew to the window to look out. I know that I will never forget what I saw then. Carl. Carl from the first floor. Lying dead on the ground. He had jumped from the top story of our eight story building. God, he was white. His skin was so very white. And his skull was split. All of his blood drained out of his head while I stood there and watched. I didn't look away. I watched for a long time—the whole time until the ambulance came and the paramedics worked on him and he was finally taken away.

They had tried to revive him. That made me so angry, so very, very angry. I mean, he was dead and I kept thinking, "Why not let him die?" But they had to attempt to revive him, I guess. So they tried for about 15 minutes. But he was dead. I had known it as soon as I saw him. I mean, he was so white. And I watched his blood drain out of his head. God, a lot has happened to me since then. Suicide certainly affects more people than just the person who dies.

I mean, I was only 19. What did I know about any of this? I was very young. I didn't know what the hell was going on. I was always very old for my age, but I was only 19! I can understand why Carl did it. I now know what his issues were. You see, he was having a really bad semester. He was not doing well academically. He was involved with alcohol and drugs. He was having difficulty with his parents. His grades were not great. He was generally feeling a lot of stress. Not to mention that his girlfriend had broken up with him just a few days before he died. Basically all the signs of suicide were there. From what I know now (I present workshops on suicide and am much more familiar with the topic than I was then), Carl's was a textbook case of suicidal behavior.

First the stress. He went on a 24-hour binge after the breakup during which he drank a lot of alcohol. I'm fairly certain that he used some marijuana and pills too. After the binge, Carl got calm and sober and remained in that state for about one day. Then he began to give away his belongings—he gave his tapes and posters to some of the people on his floor, and he even gave away his television. The next day, he wigged out again. He had been drink-

*ing and he got a little violent. He radiated back and forth be-
tween two rooms in the residence hall all night. He was agitated
and eventually began screaming nonsensical things to his friends.
He was really acting out his stress. Finally, he ran out of the
room. His two friends paused for a minute and then followed, but
Carl had beaten them onto the elevator. He went to the eighth
and top floor of the building. When he got off the elevator, he
went directly to the window in a lounge where two women were
studying. Carl stood at the window and asked the women, "Do
you dare me?" The women did not answer and Carl jumped
through the screen. That's when I heard the noise of him hitting
the ground.*

*I'm a firm believer that people should make their own choices.
And from my friendship with an RA in the building, I learned all
of these details. But while this knowledge helped me understand
Carl and the reasons why he died, it doesn't make me any less
angry. I believe, really believe, that Carl wanted to die. I mean,
he didn't make any noise when he fell—no scream, nothing. All
of his actions leading up to the suicide make it clear to me that
he really did want to die. And I've been suicidal myself. After
Carl's death, as a matter of fact. Having been there, I know how
a person thinks when suicidal and it's not the same person. When
you choose death, it's not even really your choice. But why did
he have to choose a kind of death that was so angry, so really
horrible, really bad?*

Anger Toward the Victim

*I was very mad at him, very mad. For six months afterwards,
when I closed my eyes I saw his body on the ground. Why didn't
he make it neat and use pills or something? Why this way? I mean,
I'm big on people making their own choices, but I cannot understand why he chose that way to die. He made, actually forced us
all to go through so much by being so public and gruesome with
his death. It wasn't at all easy for us to deal with. The two wom-
en who were in the lounge when Carl jumped both left school.
One left the week following his death. And Mike, another student,
was completely wigged out. As for his roommate, he read at the
memorial service. He was a journalism major and he wrote for
the school newspaper, so it wasn't surprising that his speech was
very effective. But the suicide was really hard for him. He expressed his anger at the service through his speech. He talked
about how he had enjoyed having Carl for a roommate, but he*

could find no reason for his death. His speech included the line, "He died friendless with friends all around him . . ." It was clear that he was angry and frustrated at Carl for not giving him a chance to help. It just seemed at the time that Carl didn't have to be so hard on us.

As for me, like I said before, I was only 19. Not only wasn't I ready to deal with something like this, but I also really didn't want to deal with something like this. But Carl took away my choice to refuse to do so.

Even today, six years later, I still feel the anger. I am not angry at Carl really. I am just angry at what I had to go through. His choice of method has left me no option but to endure the aftermath of such a gruesome death. I cannot deny or forget what I heard and what I saw. He could have made it easier on me— and everyone else.

Responsibility for Other Survivors

Mike, a good friend of mine at the time (whose last name I cannot now recall!) had been studying for a midterm on the night of the suicide. He took a study break at approximately 9:30 P.M. and was looking out of a window when Carl jumped. He wasn't watching from far away. He had no warning; a body simply fell past the window he happened to be looking out of. How scary!

Not surprisingly, Mike went into shock. He simply returned to his room. He didn't tell anyone about this until Sunday morning when he finally told me. I clearly remember my reaction to the information. It was hard for me because I was flipping out on my own. I mean, I was a mess. I kept thinking about the noise; it just haunted me. And Mike's confession only provided the added stress of feeling the need to take care of this additional person.

This situation was compounded when one of Mike's friends died in a car accident after the suicide. James, Mike's RA and my best friend, gave Mike a message and a number to call concerning this woman. By coincidence, I just happened to be in the room at the time. Poor Mike was excited because he thought that this friend had called him to talk, but James told him he didn't think it was good news. After some frustrations in trying to get through to her, he finally found out that she had died.

The payphone was in the hallway. Mike put the phone back on the receiver and walked into the room. He came straight to me

*and just hung on me. He put his hands on my shoulders and just
hung on me. What was I supposed to do?*

*I don't think he chose me specifically to lean on. I just think
that I was the closest person during all of this. I was just "there."
Times of crisis can really bring people together. But for me, it
was terrible. I could not deal with the responsibility of taking care
of myself and someone else. I kept thinking that I was only 19
years old. I was very young. I didn't know what the hell was going
on. I was losing a grip on myself. Although I was mature for my
age, I was only 19! I couldn't handle it.*

Paranoia that Personal Proximity Contributes to Death

*About a week after Carl died, I began to feel normal again. I
woke up on a Sunday morning in a good mood for the first time
since the suicide. I went to lunch with my roommate and James.
While we were eating another student came over to our table and
said, "So did you guys hear?" When I asked what he was talking
about, he told us that the night before a student had fallen out of
a ninth story window in a different building on campus. The
investigation showed that this fall was accidental—he was
either going to vomit or urinate out the window, and he fell.
I just said, "Oh." Then I got up from the table and left. I went
out and walked all around. I went to see the play "Equis" and I
talked to my sister for three hours from a payphone on a street
corner. I was very, very calm. I just kept thinking, "I don't want
to deal with this. I don't know how to deal with this." Then about
a week and a half later another student died—from an overdose
this time.*

*You have to understand, I had only had one experience with
death. That was when my grandfather died. So this was all new
to me. I mean, the effect of watching a person lying on the ground
draining of blood is really traumatic. I was not prepared to deal
with it. And then two other deaths on top of it . . . After this
third death, I called my dad. I was hysterical—a crying blubber-
ing blob of a person. I just kept saying, "Everybody's dying, everybody's dying." And when Dad drove up to take me home, we
saw a really awful car accident on the highway. I couldn't handle
it. I just told Dad to keep driving. I didn't want to know. There
was death everywhere.*

And at my next two schools where I worked, there were deaths near me too. One of my RAs died. One of my residents died. I developed this panicky feelings that everywhere I went people died. It got to be a fear. It seemed just a bit too coincidental that people would start dying when I showed up someplace. I was convinced it was my proximity. I mean, one of my RAs died in the first month of school. Out of the total blue sky one day. No medical reason ever given. Tell me that's a coincidence. Every time I turned around, some other damn person had died, some other person that had some relationship to my life—even if that relationship was proximity. I'm not saying that I was or am responsible for the deaths around me. And now I see it as part of life, because wherever I go, people die. I had just come to accept that it was almost like my presence made people die.

Re-Establishing One's Own Right to Life

So here I was, a 19-year-old sophomore in college, and I had just watched the blood drain out of the head of one of my peers. This was not what I had expected from my college experience. But once it happened, it changed everything for me. Suicide makes you very existential. At least it did for me. I kept asking myself "The Big Questions: Why should I choose to live when he chose to die? Why is anyone here? What is making me stay here?" I was trying to figure out what happens before we're here, after we're here, and why we are here. I mean, I was so extremely existential, I could have written The Stranger. *Some people believe that God is how we got here, why we die, and where we go. I'm not a believer. I do believe in a higher power, but not God necessarily. And so I questioned and questioned and questioned. I wanted to figure out the answers to all of these questions.*

I went to my father's house after the third death. His home is a very peaceful place that's by a pond. I spent that weekend taking a lot of walks and doing a lot of thinking. Carl's death really made me question what it's all for. Eventually when I was down by the pond, I finally cried. Wow . . . it's amazing to me that when I remember those moments by the pond tears still come to my eyes. I don't cry a lot. And I didn't cry a lot during this whole period. It's just that it was at that time by the pond that I finally said good-bye. I said good-bye to all three of the men who had died within those three weeks, but especially to Carl because he had been the first one, and his death had been so by choice, so angry, and so horrible.

During this time by the pond, I finally came to accept the fact that I was alive and that it was alright that I was alive. "The Answer" I came to conclude regarding my "Big Questions" was: "It's alright that I'm here and it's okay that Carl did what he did." This realization was incredibly comforting to me. It's not that it eliminated any of my anger. It just allowed me to let go of wondering why we're here in the first place and accept that maybe it doesn't matter why. It's just okay. And it was also okay that I was still alive and, as Carl had chosen to die, I had chosen to live. I've already said that I'm big on people making their own choices, and I mean that. And so I finally realized that my choice not to end my life was an alright choice too. My living was okay.

Making Meaning

Here I am—at my fourth institution of higher education—in my third month as a student affairs professional this time. No more student for me. And really for the first time since Carl's suicide, I've been able to detach myself from a death. Two actually. A student here died recently while in surgery. She lived in the same residence hall complex I live and work in. But I feel very removed from her death. I don't think my proximity is a factor at all. And another student committed suicide less than three weeks ago. While suicide will probably always stir up some strong emotions for me, I again feel amazingly remote from the whole situation. But it has been a long road in getting to this point . . .

I remember how after Carl died my friends and I used to have all of these exploratory discussions. We tried to define death and to relate to it. My big issue was what happens to people when they die. It's funny though, I would discuss "it" (the suicide) with anyone and everyone who wanted to talk about it. But I would not talk about myself and what a mess I was. I was very good at ignoring the relationship between the event of the suicide and the impact it was having on me. I often felt the frustration of having to deal with so much heavy stuff when I was so young, but I didn't look at all at what the process of recovery or understanding was for me.

James was wonderful. We were very close friends and he was my major support person. I processed my issues with him and he processed his issues with me. I experienced a delayed reaction in dealing with the situation though. And as the other deaths oc-

curred, I couldn't deal with it all, so I let in little pieces at a time. And James was there for all of that. He really tried to help me make sense of everything.

I think that whenever somebody dies, you feel sadness for everyone you've known who's died—or at least I do. All previous deaths play into each later death. Maybe that's why old people cry so much at funerals, because they've had so many deaths in their pasts. Anyway, when Carl died, I had only dealt with the death of my grandfather. He died right before my high school graduation. For me, the issue of death is the same. I had been very close to all of my grandparents. They were a huge part of my life. When my grandfather died, I didn't express a lot. I wasn't sure how I felt. And if I did know how I felt, I had no idea how to express that. Likewise, after Carl died, I had no idea how I felt, what I should do, or how to express what was happening for me. I didn't have any idea what it all meant.

Needless to say, I've had a lot of experiences with death since then. Too many. And I've probably thought about all of these issues much more than the average person does. My uncle died this past September, right after I started feeling somewhat acclimated to my new job. I went to his funeral, and it was the first time in my life that I was able to grieve openly and share feelings with others. I felt really good about not keeping my feelings bottled up. This is a very new thing for me, attained, I believe, through experience and age.

So while I can now look back on the past six years and see the progress I've made in dealing with death and my own feelings, I don't think dealing with suicide—or Carl's suicide—will get any easier. It really helps me to still have James to talk to though. We aren't as close as we used to be, but it's just nice to know that someone else remembers. But this God damn weather will always make me think of it. In the autumn I will always be reminded. It's weird sometimes how it totally comes back. It really affects me still.

And I also get very frustrated with the way television shows depict people falling off of buildings. Usually on television, there is little sound, just a "thump." Certainly not a huge man with a handful of baseball bats. And when the camera shot looks down on the fallen people, they look the same as they did before the fall or the jump. They are lying in a graceful position, there is no blood, and their color remains the same. Nothing like Carl— nothing true to life. No white skin, no blood, no noise. It just bothers me how unrealistic the portrayals are. Because of this, *very few people can really understand what it's like to witness what I witnessed.*

I now present workshops on suicide. Someone asked me once why I do this and I responded that I want to save the world from dying. I was just joking then, but it is kind of true. Having been close to suicide myself, I understand what it's like and how people think in that state. But I also know that people can be helped out of that. I see it as my responsibility, and the responsibility of others, to help people who show signs of suicidal behavior by getting them help—if they are mentally willing. Then if people decide to die, more power to them. It comes backs to making choices again and again. If someone is in a stable mental condition and decides to take his or her life, that's a personal prerogative. If that is what someone has to do, I can try to be understanding.

I do, however, maintain strong feelings about the method of suicide. When I was suicidal, I had planned out my method. It was going to be a very private suicide. I would never jump from a window. It just isn't fair to make other people have to deal with your choices. And when you jump from a window, that's exactly what you do. So, I can try to be understanding of someone's choice to end his or her life, but I would appreciate if people would try to be understanding of me when they decide how they are going to do that.

Soon after Carl's suicide, an alternative school newspaper printed a tasteless full page ad that pictured a yellow traffic sign which read, "Caution: Falling Student Zone" and pictured a stick figure falling from a building. I could not get over the insensitivity of the people who printed this—their mockery of such a serious situation. A group of us wrote a letter to the newspaper to let them know how insensitive they were and how much that hurt us. But I remember thinking that the people who were involved with this ad didn't know what I was feeling. They didn't have any idea. They didn't experience it.

And now, six years later, I understand a little better what I was feeling then and what I feel now. I can actually relinquish myself from any influence in the recent deaths at my present institution. I can present workshops on suicide and separate myself from the issue without difficulty. And I can tell my whole story and see the value in my experience. I have been through a lot. And I've learned a lot. But it certainly hasn't been easy. How that October night and a student named Carl changed my life.

Conclusion

Whenever a person takes his or her own life, survivors are faced with many questions, fears, and emotions. Typically, traditional-aged college students (i.e., 18–22) are at a stage in life when they are planning their futures, developing intimate friendships, and enjoying what they may believe to be the end of their youth. This sensitive time is also strongly influenced by peers. While it is imperative to realize that each survivor will experience a very personal and unique griefwork process, much can be learned from the reactions and needs of this respondent as student affairs educators prepare to handle potential responses.

The anger this respondent felt toward the victim is to be expected. Because suicide is a taboo topic in our culture, it is infrequently talked about and little understood. Survivors struggle to empathize with the plight of a victim and be supportive of his or her choice to commit suicide. Student affairs educators should allow students to discuss these feelings of anger and condone their validity, thus inhibiting the transformation of anger to guilt. Discussions about resentment toward the deceased should include an acknowledgement of the right of the victim to make personal choices. While not agreeing with the choice for suicide, if they can respect the autonomy of the individual victim, they may better accept the tragedy.

The respondent's inability and unwillingness to assist other students through this tragedy has implications for student affairs. As students (resident assistants included) attempt to meet their needs at this difficult time, they may not be able to manage the added responsibility for others' well-being. The assistance in griefwork that many will require may need to be provided by student affairs educators available and prepared to handle a range of reactions. They can facilitate discussion groups of students who come together and share their thoughts and feelings. For individual attention, survivors can be referred to counseling or campus ministry. A memorial service may be useful for students to put closure to the tragedy as well as recognize the effect of the death on the community. These steps are useful ones in helping students understand and express their emotions, individually and communally, without leaning too heavily upon each other.

The respondent's paranoia that her presence was a factor in the deaths of others provides a valuable forewarning for student affairs staff. While the occurrence of multiple deaths on campus can lead to this reaction, professionals need to be aware that numerous deaths in the student's family or off-campus relations may foster a similar response. While impossible to judge how long this paranoia will last (almost six years for this respondent), it is important to recognize that this is a real fear and will not simply dissipate. Counseling sessions and other opportunities for discussion may allow students to face and overcome this paranoia.

As exemplified by this respondent, the struggle with existential grief is a difficult and painful one. Students may attempt to revalidate their own reasons and rights for living. They may compare their lives with others to find value in their existence. Student affairs educators can assist in this process by affirming the worth of each individual survivor and engaging in discussion about existential issues. Survivors need to understand that there are no certain answers to all their questions. They may have to accept the ambiguity of life and the different choices others make.

Student affairs educators must be prepared for assisting in the postvention process. Those professionals with no experience or training in facilitating griefwork may not be ready to successfully assist survivors or understand their own reactions. Training workshops to prepare educators for a successful suicide can include signs of grief, expected reactions to suicide, methods of facilitating necessary dialogue between grieving members of the community, protocols for administrative action, institutional referral systems, and how staff can work as a team to care for themselves and others. This knowledge before the fact will help make the postvention process more effective for students and staff alike.

Shneidman (1985) wrote that:

> Grief and mourning can have the effect of reducing a well-functioning child or adult to a howling and bereft person, to an almost animal-like creature. But even at those very same moments, the grief-stricken person displays what is also the most humanlike of all his characteristics: the need and capacity for social, personal, and loving relationships and bonds. (p. 55)

Student affairs educators can facilitate these "social, personal, and loving relationships" between students, faculty, and staff by providing opportunities for these bonds to form. This situation creates an awareness about the effect the tragedy has on the larger community as well as allows students to understand their griefwork. The less survivors feel misunderstood and alone, the less painful their grieving process will be. As community builders, student affairs educators can have a significant impact on individual students' recovery as well as that of the entire campus community.

References

American Council on Education. (1937). *The student personnel point of view*. Washington, D.C.: Publisher.

LaGreca, A. J. (1988). Suicide: Prevalence, theories, and prevention. In H. Wass, F. M. Berardo, & R. A. Neimeyer (2nd ed.) (Eds.), *Dying: Facing the facts* (pp. 229–255). Washington, D.C.: Hemisphere Publishing Corporation.

Range, L. M., & Martin, S. K. (1990). How knowledge of extenuating circumstances influences community reactions toward suicide victims and their bereaved families. *OMEGA, 21*(3), 191–198.

Range, L. M., Goggin, W. C., & Steeded, K. K. (1988). Perception of behavioral contagion of adolescent suicide. *Suicide and life-threatening behavior, 18*(4), 334–341.

Shneidman, E. S. (1985). Some thoughts on grief and mourning. *Suicide and life-threatening behavior, 15*, 51–55.

Stephenson, J. S. (1985). *Death, grief, and mourning*. New York, NY: The Free Press.

Van Der Wal, J. (1989). The aftermath of suicide: A review of empirical evidence. *OMEGA, 20*(2), 149–168.

Webb, N. B. (1986). Before and after suicide: A preventive outreach program for colleges. *Suicide and life-threatening behavior, 16*, 469–480.

4

The Language of Acquaintance Rape

Melissa Regan

In her landmark book, *Against Our Will: Men, Women and Rape*, Susan Brownmiller (1975) was among the first researchers to examine systematically the reality of rape in society. She asserted that "all rape is an exercise in power" (p. 256), and thus started the process to dispel common misconceptions about rape. Unfortunately, it is difficult to completely dispel myths that have persisted in society. Therefore, we must continue to examine the issue of rape as well as combat the stereotypes that perpetuate these acts. Efforts to decrease rape are crucial for student affairs administrators especially as acquaintance rape continues unabated on college campuses (Baier, Rosenzweig, & Whipple, 1991; Finley & Corty, 1993).

The purposes of this chapter are to define rape and acquaintance rape, present a review of the history of rape, and address socialization and explore the languages developed as a result. The chapter also discusses implications for student affairs educators about rape, acquaintance rape, and the differing treatment of this subject by men and women.

Literature Review

The legal definition of rape differs from state to state and defies exactness because the traditional legal definition of rape (i.e., "male-female forced vaginal intercourse") was broadened by efforts of people in the women's movement to achieve gender neutrality, increase the chances of conviction, and encompass a wider array of sexually assaulting behaviors (Bohmer & Parrot, 1993, p. 4). Although males and females can be the victims of rape, this chapter focuses on the most common occurrence of rape which involves a female victim (Bostwick, DeLucia-Waack, & Watson, 1995). In the context of this chapter, rape is defined as "forcing a woman to have sex without consent and threatening a woman in order to obtain intercourse" (Cook, 1995, p. 186). This definition specifies an action as rape regardless of whether or not the assailant and the victim knew each other prior to the rape. The types of force involved during rape include physical violence, coercion or threat of harm to the victim (Adams & Abarbanel, 1988; Baier, Rosenzweig, & Whipple, 1991).

The statistics about rape are alarming. In the United States, while a rape is formally reported every six minutes, only a fraction of rapes are ever reported. While the reported number of rapes and sexual assaults varies widely due to divergent definitions and unreported incidences, estimates for number of rapes among college students do exist. In a survey conducted by Baier, Rosenzweig, and Whipple (1991), "14.6% of the respondents indicated that they had been forced into intercourse or another sexual act" (p. 310). In terms of attempted rape, 18.8% of the women and 10.4% of the heterosexual students surveyed reported this type of victimization (p. 316).

> Until recently, many people thought college campuses were safe environments for women. The little concern that existed for women's safety on campus was limited to stranger rapes, though these assaults are comparatively uncommon compared to women's victimization by men they know. (Belknap & Erez, 1995, p. 156)

College campuses have become the locations of an increased number of acquaintance rapes (Gallagher, Harmon, & Lingenfelter, 1994). Date rape refers "specifically to sexual victimization which occurs on a date or at a college function" (p. 158). Since approximately one-third of college males reported that they would rape women if they knew they would not get caught (Belknap & Erez,

1995), the high rate of violence against campus women is not surprising.

Regardless of the changes in societal perceptions and frequency of rape, one element has remained constant; women are predominantly the victims with men as the offenders (Belknap & Erez, 1995; Bostwick, DeLucia-Waack, & Watson, 1995). This point is not to discount that men are sometimes rape victims or that women rape other women, but factually the majority of rapes are crimes by men against women (Brownmiller, 1975).

Until recently, the popularity of rape myths and widespread misunderstanding about the motivation behind rape have been rampant in society. In the face of increased information women continue to battle the ignorance and historic misconceptions that people hold about rape. Many still believe that rape occurs in dark alleys or when someone jumps out of the bushes and places a knife to the woman's throat. As acquaintance rape is acknowledged as a crime, an entirely different set of prejudices must be confronted. For instance, many believe that a woman cannot be raped by someone she knows; that if she tried hard enough she could have gotten away; that she may be lying about the action really being rape; or that she must have led him on. Each of these statements contains the implication that the crime was the woman's fault—she was responsible. Men and women must begin to educate themselves and others that women who are raped are not responsible for the rapists' actions.

Methodology

Research in this study was conducted using constructivist inquiry (Guba & Lincoln, 1989) into the socialization of undergraduate students concerning rape. Data were collected through interviews with two current undergraduates, one male and one female. To examine the language these students use when talking about sex and acquaintance rape, I asked each student a series of questions about the influence of socialization on their attitudes, social life at their university, sex and acquaintance rape. Their responses were analyzed using the constant comparative method (Lincoln & Guba, 1985) to tease out overlapping themes, differences in language, and commonalities. The languages used by the respondents are presented in the case study in a contrasting format (e.g., male and female voices) to dramatically illustrate the differences in socialization.

The reader should note that the respondents were not college students disconnected from training and education about issues such as rape. These two students were resident assistants who had participated in training programs designed to increase understanding about critical campus issues such as sexual assault. In fact, these students represented the para-professional staff members asked to facilitate the education of non-staff residents on issues such as AIDS, diversity, sexual assault, and other sensitive issues.

Case Study

The Languages of Socialization

The woman I interviewed had the following to say about society and the consequences of premarital sex:

> *I think there's a lot of changes happening in our society, especially because of the ERA [Equal Rights Amendment] movement and feminist movement. There was a time when women were to stay virgins until they were married and that was the thing to do and men wanted to marry virgins.*
>
> *I think sex was still an issue, I think young people still wanted it, but it wasn't socially acceptable to do it. And it wasn't desirable to be a woman and not a virgin if you wanted to be married. It was a prerequisite for marriage—virginity. And it seems like sex didn't really have as many of the same problems then because sex had its defined roles. Sex was in a marital relationship and you didn't play until you were married.*

Similarly, the male respondent shared his thoughts about the socialization process:

> *I think it's that guys are supposed to be in charge and the women are supposed . . . It's kind of tough because women are supposed to be everything. They are supposed to be feminine, yet in a way, aggressive, to succeed at the same time they are supposed to be soft, and . . . I don't know . . .*
>
> *I can see where it would be confusing for women, but it seems like they are brought up to remain virgins until they are married. Guys are suppose to lose their virginity as soon as possible. [It's] just [that] the numbers don't balance out. I think a lot of girls*

are afraid of sex because they see it as bad, that's part of it. But I think a lot of girls are confused and don't know whether they are doing the right thing. The guys don't have that guilt in any way. This is just something they are supposed to do—so guys can do anything.

I think acquaintance rape and these attitudes are just symptoms of women not being treated as equals on a lot of levels. [In] business settings, or whatever, they are treated as objects and not as people and I think they get this learned instinct to be an object and not a person and I think that's why these situations arise.

In her book, *In a Different Voice*, Carol Gilligan (1982) explored the socialization process of boys and girls. She determined that girls are more concerned with maintaining the relationships in their lives whereas boys are more concerned with the assertion of their independence. Women are taught to be polite and passive so as not to disrupt their relationships with others. Boys, on the other hand, are taught to be aggressive through team sports and competition (Hughes & Sandler, 1987). Not surprisingly, therefor, boys bring these assumptions and expectations to the college campus where they have many freedoms regarding dating.

The Nature of Social Life on Campus

Given the information noted above and the themes unfolding in this research, college women are in a precarious position. Traditional aged college students are often away from their parents for the first time and can be unsophisticated in handling new situations (Chickering & Reisser, 1991). Skills balancing independence and security have yet to be developed and they are likely to test the limits of their new freedoms (Ehrhart & Sandler, 1985).

Many college men try to prove themselves through sexual activities (Warshaw, 1988). This bravado among college men may be amplified by the assumption that college women are sexually liberated, sexually active, and want sex (Ehrhart & Sandler, 1985). In these situations, clear communication between men and women is essential. However, given the learned patterns of behavior for both genders, the nature of college campuses, and myths surrounding acquaintance rape, educators fight an uphill battle to encourage honest and open communication among sexual partners.

When asked about the nature of social life at the university, the female respondent replied:

> *There's always the bars. But I think one of the biggest places is the fraternities because if you don't have an i.d. [identification] you can always get into a fraternity. Well, not always, but . . . They are not that difficult to get into and I think you see a lot of underage drinking going on there. The guys go to parties to pick up girls. Girls go to parties to get picked up. Drinking is always a factor in there. I wouldn't say that drinking is the main reason for going to a fraternity party because I think people who are solely interested in drinking stay home. But it's the guys who want to be drinking and looking at girls and picking them up, and the girls who want to be looked at and picked up that go to the fraternities. Unless they have friends at the fraternity those girls are usually not approachable by other guys so it really doesn't matter. I think a woman puts off an air—either she puts off the air that she's vulnerable, or she puts off the air like, "don't touch me, don't come near me," and "try it if you can," so I think it's a big game.*

The female respondent also asserted:

> *It's the attitude you go into a fraternity or a bar with. Guys know the difference between women who are "off limits" and those who are interested in possibly hooking up. And those who aren't interested in even talking. You see girls who obviously "dolled themselves up" to look really cute and they want guys to talk to them, or try to pick them up. Or women who get dressed up and their purpose is to have sex. There's an attitude that you put forth that guys can sense.*

The male respondent also related his perspective about campus social life:

> *I think it's sad that girls have to be careful, but I think sometimes they are not careful enough. Because when they do drink they are going to become easy victims. It's too bad it's like that. A guy can pretty much go and get totally plastered and he is reasonably safe, at least in that sense. But a girl does not have that and I think they need to know how dangerous things can really be.*
> *I think if you are at a party it is easier to go up to someone*

who is totally plastered because if they reject you it isn't such a big deal. But if you go up to someone who is sober, that is going to take a lot more work on your part. Plus, when girls are intoxicated they are hanging all over, so it's real easy, you just have to walk over there. It's not going to take a lot of effort for him to get her to do whatever. But on the other hand I know guys who will see drunk girls and not want anything to do with it. I think they are in the minority.

He continued by saying:

Fraternities are meat markets. I was at a party and it was like throw out your hook. It was girls everywhere and guys trying to pick them up and girls trying to pick up guys. That's pretty much the way it is. You go there, and that is what everyone is doing and that is what everyone is thinking about and that is why they are there, I guess. And that's not wrong, but that's what I think they are like.

The Language of Rape

Any exploration about rape needs to involve an examination of the way men talk about sex and women (Beneke, 1982). In *Metaphors We Live By*, George Lakoff and Mark Johnson (1980) discussed the language patterns used to conceive of, live in, and experience the world. In a metaphor we understand and experience one object or idea in terms of another.

Metaphors may create realities for us, especially social realities. A metaphor may thus be a guide for future action. Such actions will, of course, fit the metaphor. This will in turn reinforce the power of the metaphor to make experience coherent. In this sense, metaphors can be self fulfilling prophecies (Lakoff & Johnson, 1980, p. 156).

Beneke (1982) listed metaphors that men use when referring to sex and women. His examples included:

1. Sex is achievement.
   "I'd like to **make it** with her."
   "Maybe I'll **get** her into bed."
   "You didn't have to **work very hard** to **get into her pants**."
2. Sex is a game.
   "I hope I **score** tonight."

"I **struck out** with her."
3. Sex is war.
   "He's always **hitting on** women."
   "I tried to get her into bed, but got **shot down**."
4. Sex is performance.
   "You were **great** last night."
   "I got **rave reviews in bed**."
   "He's **good in bed**."
5. Sex is a commodity.
   "Why should a man rape if he can **get it for free**?"
   "She wouldn't **give me any**."
   "I've been **getting it regularly** lately."
   "Do you know any **available** women?"
6. Women are objects.
   "She's a cute **thing**."
   "Check **that** out."
   "She likes to **flaunt it**."
7. Women are animals.
   "She is a nice **chick**."
   "She works as a Playboy **bunny**."
   "She's real **foxy**."
   "She's really a **dog**"
   "What a **bitch**!"
8. Women are children.
   "Do you like the **girls** at the office?"
   "Janice is our **playmate** of the month!"
   "Hey, **baby**!"

These are just a few of the examples listed in Beneke's book which serve to illustrate how men may metaphorically structure their experience of themselves, women, and sex.

Many men have used or are familiar with at least one of these phrases; men and women are socialized not to consider the implications of these metaphors and remarks (Beneke, 1982). It is unnerving to note that these examples include four basic themes: status, hostility, control, and dominance. These four themes are often noted as part of rapists' motivations. While not every man is a rapist, the vocabulary of rape myths is incorporated into his reality. For example, the male respondent relayed this story:

[The men on his floor] always talk about sex. On the weekends they act like they are under a lot of pressure. I think a lot

*of them came to college with the idea that they were going to
drink and have sex all the time or something. They are not so
much looking for relationships as they are for scores. That's what
they always talk about. One incident I remember really vividly,
about three weeks into the semester.*

*Last semester, I was going to sleep and I heard some of the
guys outside talking. And I go outside to hear what it is about
and one of the guys is going, "Hey, Dave, Mike [pseudonyms]
put the puck in the net!" And I'm like, "What are you guys talking about?" And he goes, "He put the puck in the net with Sue."
And it clicked on and they proceeded to tell me the story. Two of
the guys on my floor were in these two girls' room and one of
the guys left and one of the girls was like, "Does he like me?"
And so the other one proceeded to tell her this story to kind of
coax her into whatever, and then Mike came back and as he said,
"Put the puck in the net." Then they all came downstairs and
were all **high-fiving** and treating it like it was a puck in the net
or something. They were just going off—it was like a **pep rally** or
something. He never spoke to her again. I've never seen something so cold, it was just a score and nothing more.*

The woman I interviewed said:

*Sex is a real big thing up on the guys' floors. I've gotten to be
pretty good friends with some of the guys and they know I'm **off
limits**. So, they joke with me about sex and I think I am in a
good position up there because I am learning a lot from them
because they are not trying to **pick me up** because they know I
have no interest in them. They do joke around with me a lot about
sex. I go up there a lot and there is this one guy who is pretty
cocky and he thinks he is pretty hot. He's always going, "C'mon,
baby, you know you want me." It's a joke, but it sort of shows
the mentality too. It's like the guys have something to give us and
we have something to lose, and that is just the way they say it.
For instance, men talk about **getting it**, that's their purpose—to
get it. Women talk about **losing it**—losing their virginity.*

She continued:

*I've been in a room talking with some guys and this guy came
in and he had just had a sexual experience and this was strange
for this guy, it was a new thing, and I was immediately ushered
out of the room so they could have a **pow-wow** and talk about it.*

*I think the guys put a lot of pressure on the guys who don't have sex a lot—it's kind of a status symbol—whether you're **getting** or **not getting** it. But at the same time there are guys who aren't like that because they choose to be and there are men who aren't like that because they are **geeks**, and they just can't seem to **get** a girl no matter **how hard they try**. And the guys who are trying and not getting it really get ragged on. They do. But at the same time the guys support them and try to set these guys up with possible women. They rag on them, but they support them too. It's sort of a weird phenomenon. There are guys who have girlfriends and they are totally respected.*

The peer group also influences dating behaviors in other ways. According to the male student:

*Any girl who, in any way, pisses any one of them off they are called a **clam** or a **dumb clam**. I think if they don't have sex with a girl then they get a negative attitude about her and are always talking about her. They are very appearance oriented. If a girl doesn't look a certain way usually they tear her to shreds. I think it's a group thing. When you're with a group of guys and an ugly girl walks by, you have to make a big deal about it. But I think one-on-one they wouldn't say anything. They are under a lot of pressure.*

*If a guy starts dating someone he immediately comes under scrutiny and if the girl doesn't measure up a lot of times he won't keep seeing her. There was one guy who was going out with this girl, well he fooled around with her, and the next day the guys said "oh, you were **goggling**—what were you doing with that **beast**?" So right after that he didn't see her anymore. I'm sure their comments had something to do with his change of heart.*

In the meantime, women have a role to play in the campus social life as well. The female student said:

I don't hear [about sex] as much from the women. They don't talk as openly about it. See, it's like for guys it's okay, it's like their role to be the sexual aggressor. And for women it's not . . . I am sure women talk about it, but they don't talk about it like men do. It's not public knowledge on a women's floor, but it is on a guys floor. If someone got it last night, you know it if you live on a guys floor, but for a woman it's not something that people go spreading around and only close friends know about it.

There's this one girl on my floor who a lot of girls on my floor were concerned about because she was always going home with a different guy. She was also rushing a sorority. What bugged them was they kept saying to her, "Can't you see these guys are using you?" And she said back, "Well, I am using them too." It was almost a naivete about her, she didn't realize what she was saying. I don't think she was really using them, she just thought that was the way to be accepted and the way to be liked by the opposite sex. So anyway the situation was never resolved because she continued to go on and believe these guys truly liked her and having sex with them was ok because she was getting just as much out of it as they were. That could be the case, but I don't know. I guess I just don't see many women actually believing that.

Similarly, the male respondent said the following about the women he encountered:

It's funny because when a girl does it, she's getting around. I've known a couple of girls who will just do whatever. Some talk real explicitly like, "I'm gonna get him" but that is very few. I think it would actually be better if more women thought like that. If they were more mature. I think they always feel victimized by sex. Something is always happening to them. Whereas they can empower themselves and go and have a relationship and be in control, but I don't think a lot of them do that. I think they just want to take a backseat and let the guys lead them around. That's my impression.

But there are girls who will use guys. Sometimes I hear them talking and they are a lot like guys in their attitude, like, "I'm gonna pick up this babe." I think it pales in comparison to guys, but I think they still do it to some degree.

He continued:

Guys will just as soon call some girl a slut if she sleeps around, but girls are especially bad to each other about that. Guys talk about other guys doing whatever, but when a girl gets around, the other girls are just all over her, always giving her shit. But they really do that. I think we contribute to it too, but I don't think they are helping themselves with that kind of attacking, and they do it a lot.

Acquaintance Rape Education

Since both respondents are members of the resident assistant program, I asked them about the education the university provides students about acquaintance rape and rape. The male responded:

A couple of my guys went to a program on [acquaintance rape]. The program went okay, but one of the guys raised a point. They had been talking about if a guy has been seeing a girl for a long time and they've had sex and they have sex again and she calls it rape. He said he didn't think it was fair. He kinda got lashed out at by the girls in the room. The program wasn't that successful in that regard. It became women against men.

In response to a question about whether it would be possible to present the topic in such a way that it did not put the men against the women, he replied:

I think it can be done. It's kind of tough. I don't think it's good to have an all-guys forum on rape and an all-girls forum on rape. I think it's important to have both [present].

One of the RAs showed "The Accused" and then had a discussion after that. I think the movie kind of had the girls so shocked and upset. I don't think people realize what a graphic situation [rape] is, and I think it is good to show that. I think programs should really talk about it in explicit terms and say, "here are the facts."

The female respondent, also an RA and the victim of an acquaintance rape herself, offered her opinion about campus rape education:

As educators we need to be putting on programs that aren't statistics-oriented, but that are people-oriented. I gave a program where I told my story. After an introduction I told my story and opened myself up to these girls, these women, and just said "you can ask me any question, painful or embarrassing." You know, I had probably heard it before and I could give them real answers to real questions and solve some of their misconceptions. Now they have someone to associate with the words "acquaintance rape." They know I don't dress in tight skirts and hang out in bars and, you know, do all those stereotypical things that they think a woman who is raped was doing so therefore she got raped.

I think we need to do some image breaking and some educating and I don't think programs that try to scare people are very effective, but programs where people just like me can share experiences with others. I know just from that program I received ten phone calls from girls who had been raped, others who weren't sure, and some who just wanted to find out more.

It is a frustration for me right now because I want to do a program on acquaintance rape in our hall but my other staff members are just like "no, we hear about this all the time." But they don't understand that people don't really know enough about it and that they have so many misconceptions.

She continued:

We need to educate men and women. We need to educate women to say no and mean it. And we need to educate men to not accept a sketchy situation [but] to find out exactly what the woman's feelings are.

Conclusions and Interpretations

Through this research I was astonished to learn that these two resident assistants were not as educated in this area as I had thought they might be. My initial concern about the respondents giving me the answers I "wanted" or was expecting to hear from resident assistants was not realized. Instead, they provided me with candid, first-hand accounts which I believe reflected their experiences in the residence halls. The respondents provided me with more information than could possibly be included within this case study. They raised some interesting and essential questions about the education provided to students about acquaintance rape and rape.

Both respondents expressed their frustration with date rape being just a "hot topic" that students were tired of hearing about. They were concerned with presenting information to students to make them realize the realities of college life and the possibility of acquaintance rape, but had conflicting ideas about the manner in which to go about it.

Implications for Student
Affairs Administrators

The statistics surrounding incidents of acquaintance rape on campus are startling. Student affairs educators need to evaluate the ways they communicate with students about this issue. Students and educators alike need to return to the basic elements of relationships and combat the prevalent stereotypes on campus and within society. Resident assistants as well as full-time hall staff should be thoroughly trained in this area. They should serve as role models to the students on the hall as well as create an environment in which people of both sexes, and of different sexual orientations, can feel comfortable with their sexuality. Mutual respect can be fostered and encouraged while the realities of acquaintance rape are discussed.

Students need to be made aware of the possibility of acquaintance rape as early in the first semester as possible. In that way, the university takes a proactive stance instead of waiting for incidents to occur before confronting the issue. The topic can be handled in a manner that need not create anxiety, but will open the channels of communication between students, men and women, from the start of their college careers. This early intervention is an effective way to break through some of the myths and stereotypes about rape. Men may realize that their expectations about women are unrealistic. Women may recognize that they are in control of their lives and may need to take a more assertive stance than they may have been brought up to believe they should.

Summary

Given the literature reviewed and interviews conducted with these students, it was clear that socialization, campus culture, and language use are contributing factors in the increased incidents of acquaintance rape. College students, given their new freedoms, expectations about sex during college, and past socialization are at a vulnerable stage in their development. They are insecure about their individuality and their abilities to relate effectively with other people sexually. This insecurity is combined with the incredible amount of peer pressure from individuals who are also struggling with similar issues.

College campuses are full of conflicting messages concerning sex and gender roles. A clear message needs to be sent from the campus community in as many forms as possible. According to Gager and Schurr,

> Rape is a crime which has thrived on misconceptions, prejudice, lies, indifference, and the past silence of victims. Today that silence is being broken, thanks to the courage and sacrifice of women acting alone and together. Women's voices are now being heard. They are determined to remain silent no longer. (1976, p. 291)

Rape is not just a woman's problem. Men need to help in the battle to break the silence. Student affairs educators should take the lead in this effort and begin to set the stage for change.

References

Adams, A., & Abarbanel, G. (1988). *Sexual assault on campus: What colleges can do.* Santa Monica, CA: Rape Treatment Center.

Baier, J. L., Rosenzweig, M. G., & Whipple, E. G. (1991). Patterns of sexual behavior, coercion, and victimization of university students. *Journal of College Student Development 32,* 310–322.

Belknap, J., & Erez, E. (1995). The victimization of women on college campuses: Courtship violence, date rape, and sexual harassment. In B. Fisher & J. Sloan, *Campus crime: Legal, social, and policy perspectives* (pp. 156–178). Springfield, IL: Charles C. Thomas.

Beneke, T. (1982). *Men on rape.* New York, NY: St. Martin's Press.

Bohmer, C., & Parrot, A. (1993). *Sexual assualt on campus: The problem and the solution.* New York, NY: Lexington Books.

Bostwick, T., DeLucia-Waack, J. L., & Watson, D. (1995). Perceptions of dating behaviors and reasons offered to justify date rape. *NASPA Journal, 32,* 123–129.

Brownmiller, S. (1975). *Against our will: Men, women and rape.* New York, NY: Bantam Books.

Chickering, A., & Reisser, L. (1991). (2nd ed.). *Education and identity.* San Francisco, CA: Jossey-Bass.

Cook, S. L. (1995). Acceptance and expectation of sexual aggression in college students. *Psychology of Women Quarterly, 19,* 181–194.

Ehrhart, J. K., & Sandler, B. R. (1985). Campus gang rape: Party games? Washington, DC: Project on the Status and Education of Women. Association of American Colleges.

Finley, C., & Corty, E. (1993). Rape on campus: The prevalence of sexual assault while enrolled in college. *Journal of College Student Development, 34*, 113–117.

Gager, N., & Schurr, C. (1976). *Sexual assault: Confronting rape in America.* New York, NY: Grosset E. Dunlap.

Gallagher, R. P., Harmon, W. W., & Lingenfelter, C. O. (1994). CSAO's perceptions of the changing incidence of problematic college student behavior. *NASPA Journal, 32*, 37–45.

Gilligan, C. (1982). *In a different voice.* Cambridge, MA: Harvard University Press.

Guba, E., & Lincoln, Y. (1989). *Fourth generation evaluation.* Beverly Hills, CA: Sage.

Hughes, J. O., & Sandler, B. R. (1987). Friends raping friends: Could it happen to you? Washington, DC: Project on the Status and Education of Women. Association of American Colleges.

Lakoff, G., & Johnson, M. (1980). *Metaphors we live by.* Chicago, IL: University of Chicago Press.

Lincoln, Y., & Guba, E. (1985). *Naturalistic inquiry.* Newbury Park, CA: Sage Publications.

Warshaw, R. (1988). *I never called it rape.* New York, NY: Harper and Row Publishers.

5

Picking Up the Pieces

A Case Study of the Death of a Resident

Elizabeth A. Skeffington

Students who lose a friend to an alcohol-related death require immediate attention. They comprise a unique group of individuals on a campus. An even more individualized cluster of students are those resident assistants who concurrently come to terms with the loss of a friend and serve as a key support person for others experiencing the death. As much thought and reflection must be given to the role resident assistants play in the aftermath of these tragedies as is given to the type of assistance all students receive.

A purpose of this chapter is to create a vicarious experience for the reader such that he or she might better understand alcohol-related tragedies and their effects on residence life staff. The research brings to light areas of concern for administrators who come into contact with resident assistants during an alcohol-related tragedy. It is imperative for the resident assistant to understand the role he or she fills for the students. Clearly communicated guidelines contribute to the support other students will receive from their peer serving in this helping role.

This case study reports research conducted on the experience of a traditional age male senior in a four-year public institution; it is an exemplar to be used to convey and understand the serious impact of alcohol on students. During this student's time as a resident assistant, a member of his floor died in an alcohol-related accident. The case study gives his account of the tragedy through his process of designing an art class project commemorating the death of his resident and other similar tragedies. The three dimensional design created for the art project portrays an unsettling image of the terminal effects of alcohol abuse.

The issue of alcohol use and its effects permeates college campuses with no relief in sight. A premise of this paper is that students need to move beyond emotion into action. The statistics available do not adequately convey the message that alcohol, particularly binge drinking, kills; we must rely on the experiences of individuals touched by those deaths. We must support, assist, and advise individuals affected by alcohol-related deaths.

The research summarized in this chapter presents questions for those in higher education. Administrators, faculty, and staff may identify with this student's experience and reflect on the strategies utilized in the past. Educating students about alcohol use and its life altering consequences is one of the most important aspects of serving students. Continually examining, assisting, and establishing boundaries for the RA involved in an alcohol-related tragedy are crucial aspects of serving students as well.

Literature Review

In 1990, students enrolled at 56 four-year institutions were asked through the CORE Survey Instrument, "How many times have you had five or more drinks (a drink is a bottle of beer, a glass of wine, a wine cooler, a shot of liquor, or a mixed drink) at a sitting?" This rate of consumption is considered "binge drinking." Forty-five per cent answered that they had binged one or more times in the last two weeks and 30.6 per cent answered that they had binged two or more times in the last two weeks (Presley, Mellman, & Lyerla, 1993). Effectively confronting alcohol use on college campuses means accepting the reality that an overwhelming portion of the student population chooses to drink (Jenson, Peterson, Murphy, & Emmerling, 1992). Most colleges and universities have alcohol education programs, but students still associate drinking with higher education and some die because of it.

From a study investigating how living environment, expectancies, peers, and gender influence alcohol consumption, Martin and Hoffman (1993) concluded that "Students living in fraternities, group houses, or coed residence halls had significantly higher rates of alcohol use than did students living at home with parents" (p. 209). Peers, particularly in close living environments, strongly influence and dictate other's behavior regarding alcohol consumption. In a study which examined how campus environment and peers influence student drinking, Shore and Rivers (1985) found that students' previous drinking patterns are perpetuated or discontinued based on the norms of their new college community. Two-thirds of college students begin drinking in high school; peer influence sustains this pattern or curtails it.

This chapter connects the literature concerning drinking patterns among students with the reality of an alcohol-related death. The research portrayed in the case study was conducted from the point of view of a resident assistant directly connected to the tragic death of his resident. In this way, the literature about alcohol use among students can be related to interventions by student affairs practitioners.

Methodology

Purpose of the Study

Using constructivist inquiry and emergent paradigm research (Ely, Anzul, Friedman, Garner, & Steinmetz, 1991; Guba & Lincoln, 1989), I explored a resident assistant's experience with the death of a resident. My interest in this topic emanated from the knowledge that these tragic incidents occur regularly throughout the United States. I gained insight into this resident assistant's experience to better assist students and resident assistants during alcohol-related crises.

Data Collection

The respondent was a first year resident assistant residing on a floor of male residents. He was a business major and respected student leader. The respondent, who I refer to by the pseudonym "Sean," was chosen because I knew he had experienced an alcohol-related tragedy and, in previous settings, I observed him to be a reflective and articulate individual. I felt confident that he could provide richly descriptive and interpretive insights to culminate in a case study.

During an introductory meeting, we discussed consent guidelines and established rules under which the research would proceed. These procedures included the nature of qualitative research, researcher expectations of the respondent, and respondent expectations (Lincoln & Guba, 1985). We agreed on a system for member checking; he read and edited fieldnotes to be returned to me in subsequent meetings. Interviews were the primary data collection method, but observation (e.g., viewing the art class project on display in the student center) and document analysis (e.g., a paper he wrote describing significant experiences in his life) were also used.

The data collection began with open-ended questions (Lincoln & Guba, 1985) which uncovered his views of his resident assistant role before and after the tragedy. The questions also probed the effects of the incident on the floor community. He shared the details of the student's death and his step by step response, feelings, and reactions during and after the tragedy.

Data Analysis

Open-ended questioning continued during second and third interviews. The data analysis, conducted through ongoing unitizing and categorizing of the data (Glaser & Strauss, 1967), produced several themes discussed in detail during the fourth interview. These in-depth discussions gave the respondent an opportunity to co-construct the interpretations and directly connect them to his experience. As such, the research findings are directly grounded in the data and respondent's experience.

We jointly decided to use a design he created for an art class as the organizing framework of the case study. He approved the idea of incorporating the design into the case study framework despite the fact that this approach jeopardized his confidentiality. He felt that using the design made the case study more effective and, in my words, better able to convey the emic or insider's perspective (Geertz, 1983).

The final interview was insightful as we discussed the design piece by piece to uncover its symbolic and deeper meanings. As he explained his design rationale, I made connections between that design and his painful experience with the student's death.

Trustworthiness and Authenticity

To assure a rigorous study, I employed methodological techniques to assure trustworthiness and authenticity (Lincoln & Guba, 1986).

The research obtained breadth through the use of persistent observation in the number of interviews conducted as well as the range of issues explored.

Depth was obtained through prolonged engagement activities including extensive time spent with the respondent as well as intensity of the issues explained. These techniques allowed me to establish trust with the respondent which is reflected in our joint decision to use his design as the organizing framework for the case study. The respondent trusted my understanding of how embedded the art project was in his experience with the student's death.

Final member checking was completed shortly after the final interview; the respondent had no revisions. A colleague experienced with qualitative research audited (Lincoln & Guba, 1986) the case study using an audit trail system linking the case study to the field notes.

Case Study

Prologue

The case study is written in first person to provide the reader with a vicarious experience of anger, sadness and depression. I strove to convey the respondent's individuality, personality, and experience most convincingly from this point of view. Nearly every word within the case study was spoken by the respondent during interviews. The writing style (e.g., pauses for reflection) seeks to accurately represent this individual and the manner in which he speaks.

Each section of the case study begins with a description of an aspect of the three dimensional art design. A vignette of his experience follows each description; the case study culminates with a complete unveiling of the design symbolizing the interweaving of the design and his words, the two components of the data collection. The final section of the case study conveys the respondent's thoughts as he presented the art project to his class.

Picking Up the Pieces

> *Create a three dimensional design.*
> *Use my emotion.*
> *Choose a topic I feel something for. My professor said people who create good stuff have great emotion about their subject. Oh great, I'm a business major and she wants me to feel.*

So I sit here in this lab. I think it's been about an hour. This stool has no back support. I want to keep my head down and just think. The others in the lab must be looking at me like I'm crazy but I need to feel emotion and create a design from it.

What do I feel strongly about? . . . alcohol . . .

I do feel strongly about alcohol and I've had contact with it. A couple of designs come to mind. I don't like them, they have no impact. I need emotion and out of that will come an image. I'll just sit here with my head down.

I feel like I'm entering a room, all the way deep inside, and I don't want to be here. Alcohol has had such an effect on my life and I don't even drink. It destroys lives. It's dangerous. You can't control its consequences and I'm afraid of consequences I can't control. I'm afraid of this strong force and what it can do.

I made the decision not to drink before I knew all these people who alcohol killed. Yes, I know I made the right decision, yet it sucks that all these people are gone.

Anger. . . . That's what I feel. Sadness. . . . That all this has happened. Depression . . . That all these lives have passed. It all goes deep into my stomach . . .

Why am I in this place? Who brought me here? Each student who has died put me here in this room and I think of each of them and the anger, sadness, and depression keep going through me.

I want to create something from these emotions and have it impact people. Shake them. Come on folks.

I don't just want people to look at my design and feel sad and have that be all they feel. Not a whole lot of action comes from sadness. People look at death and say wow, that's sad, and it doesn't move them to action.

Sadness translated into anger. Shattered glass. Blood on a tray. That's the image I come up with. A tall beer bottle in the center, unbroken, whole. This is how I think of alcohol. It won't break. It's very much whole. The things it can do. The lives it closely touches, it destroys, shatters. This is the center of my design, a tall beer bottle with the shiny foil wrapper still intact. Those students who died, alcohol may not have been the center of their lives, but it was the center of their deaths.

How can I convey to people that just accepting alcohol as part of society and what it does to people isn't helping? It mattered how my resident died because it should've been avoided. It matters that he's gone. At the very center is the fact that he's gone. When I pull away from that, and try to learn lessons

*from it and wonder how can it be prevented again, I just keep
coming back to the question . . . Why is he gone? I just keep
coming back to anger, sadness, depression, shattered glass, and
blood on a tray.*

The Assignment—How It All Happened

*Someone nominated me to apply for the position of resident
assistant. I don't think I would have applied for the job if someone didn't suggest it to me. Initially I thought it was a good
idea because it would provide a challenge for me. I could work
on confronting my shyness, and speaking in front of groups of
people. It was a good experience to have for life and future employment, and I liked the added responsibility that the job would
bring. I don't like sitting around, and this was a way to be involved.*

*The living environment on my floor, my first year, was awful. I
knew I could do a better job than my RA. So, I quit the tennis
team, because I already knew how to play tennis, and became an
RA to improve areas within myself that I felt the position would
challenge.*

*Being an RA is not just a job, it's a lifestyle. For me it was an
opportunity to put my values into practice, to develop and challenge them as well. I believe that I am a role model for residents
living in the building. To encourage students to focus on their
academics, I must focus on my academics. To enforce an alcohol
policy, my behavior must be consistent with the alcohol policy.
My Mom made a bet with me when I was 11. If I didn't drink
until I was 21, she would give me $500. Friends asked me if I
wanted to drink and I'd say, no I'm getting paid. It was a good
story. Yet the truth is I didn't want to drink and it was a good
excuse not to. I didn't do it for the money. The sheer thing of it
was I saw what alcohol did to my friends and I didn't like it.*

*Reflecting on the death of my resident. . . . Maybe I'm not
completely done dealing with the emotions, feelings, and thoughts
that are once again swirling in my head. I haven't thought this
deeply about this in awhile.*

Torn Pictures—The Residents

*The torn pictures, scattered throughout the design, are people
connected to those students who died. Family, friends, floormates,*

teammates. You have to really look for them within the center of the bottles. All those people who my resident left behind.

I remember being called at 2:00 A.M, while asleep at my friend's room. My hall supervisor's voice on the other end of the line telling me that one of my resident's had died. Okay, okay, okay, do you want me to come over? Hanging up the phone and sitting there and thinking, still half asleep. I called her back and asked what had happened? Next thing I knew, I was running across campus, back to my residence hall. I think it was cold outside. I don't remember feeling anything . . . I was just thinking. . . .

Who do I need to call? What do I need to do for the residents? What about his roommate? What does he need? Who should I call so they can help the residents? This is crisis management here. Helping the 34 people on my floor, well 33, was the most important thing to me.

I remember when the roommate of the resident who had died arrived back at the residence hall shortly after I did. He had been at a party. The hall supervisor and I told him that his roommate had passed away and we told him how it happened. What words do you use to say something like that? He reacted in disbelief and I asked him what he wanted to do? Did he want to go over to the hospital, call his parents, what? I kept thinking, let him make the decisions, let him decide what he needs, and I will do it.

So we went over to the hospital. He wanted to see his deceased roommate. The doctors advised against it. We started to leave and the deceased resident's parents came into the hospital. The roommate decided that he didn't want to see the parents of his deceased friend so we avoided them by going out another exit. As we left, I could hear his mother screaming. That scream made me realize that this was really happening and I was living the situation. My body felt hollow and the scream just echoed through me. I remember the screaming.

The roommate and I arrived back at the residence hall and he chose to call his parents, and tell a couple of friends what happened. Before I knew it, the news had spread throughout the floor, like news has a way of doing. Pockets of people were gathered in rooms talking about what happened. I was the floater, going from room to room and making sure everybody was okay. There wasn't much emotion put in, what I was feeling didn't matter, all these people were in crisis. I just wanted to create some calm within the turmoil. It was my job to make sure everyone was all right.

We all had to help one another. Between stops I would call my hall supervisor. We were in contact the whole time, making sure we were doing the right things and being supportive of one another.

A meeting was scheduled for the residents for the next morning. People from around campus, Residential Life, Student Activities, Counseling and Testing would be there to talk with the students about everything going on.

Finally, it was time for me to go to bed, but I didn't get much sleep.

Broken Bottles—The Deceased Student

Around the unbroken center bottle are six shorter bottles. Each is broken and shattered differently. I used a hammer. Some took a few tries. In my image, the bottles actually form people, head, shoulders, hands. Five of the bottles represent five students who had already died. One of the five represents my resident.

I remember laying in bed and all those emotions I had put on hold for the sake of my residents were allowed to resurface. All that was left to do was lay there in the dark and think. . . .

. . . I only knew him for three months. . . . He was cool, an all-American kid.

. . . Everybody liked him. . . . He was smart.

. . . He came to all the floor meetings and asked intelligent questions.

. . . He seemed like the kind of guy who you could go to with a problem and he'd give you an honest answer . . . I remember when he told me that he was pledging. I was kind of surprised, yet he liked having fun as much as anybody. And he did drink and sometimes irresponsibly. He wasn't perfect.

Just thinking that to myself makes me cringe. . . . he did drink . . .he wasn't perfect . . . Why do I judge people like that? Will I ever reach the point when I won't struggle with this? Yet, when this was all happening, it didn't matter how he died, or anything. All that mattered was that he did die, and there were a lot of people living with me who might not deal with it very well.

I had dreams that night and he was in them. Probably my unconscious mind's way of dealing with all that had happened. It was very unsettling and I can't remember what I dreamed about. I kept thinking, you don't get to mourn yet, this isn't the best time for me to mourn.

Broken Glass and Mangled Bottle Caps— Supporting the Residents

All along the base of the design, scattered around, are sharp, broken pieces of glass, and mangled bottle caps. This is turmoil. There was nothing calm about this. I needed to take care of all these folks on my floor. That is all that mattered. Each had a different amount of hurt and pain. Each was broken and cut differently. We were all in this together.

It was difficult waking everybody up the next morning to share the news. I wanted to make sure that everyone got the accurate information, for their sake and for the sake of the resident.

As the lump in my throat grew bigger and bigger, I realized I was not going to make it through the meeting. Emotions took over, I didn't do very well. I was disappointed that I broke down in front of my residents. I let myself down. This was not the way I wanted to act. I wanted to give the students accurate information, squelch rumors, not cry.

Administrators came up to me and said that it was good that I showed emotion. Now residents will realize that it is a natural response to the situation. I did want residents to feel comfortable enough to feel and express whatever emotions they were feeling, I just didn't want to be the one to do it as well. I was mission control, we were all freaked out, but I was mission control. It took three people to convince me that it was okay to show that amount of emotion in front of my residents.

I wanted so much to be viewed as the rational, calm, stable person, everyone thinks I am. I knew the residents were going to go through a lot because I had been through this before myself. My best friend committed suicide in the summer between our freshman and sophomore years of high school. The two of us played tennis every weekend and after school almost every day. He was a catcher of butterflies, a tennis player, a Huey Lewis listener, a naturalist. But most of all, he was a close friend who decided to say good-bye forever.

In a lot of ways, dealing with the death of my friend had prepared me to help the residents deal with this death. I remembered my Pastor just sitting with me in my living room. He didn't say anything, but he was there. I knew some residents would not deal well with it, and I knew others would be scared. They're going to need support.

People kept telling me that I was doing a lot. Looking back, I was too involved in the whole aftermath. Maybe I don't like ask-

ing for help. Planning the memorial service, arranging transportation to the funeral. If I didn't do it, it wouldn't get done. And I wanted to do these things for the residents.

Everyone lives in their own world and certain events have different levels of significance to each person. My resident's death consumed my world. I guess I wanted it to consume other's worlds like it did mine. Administrators definitely came up to me and told me they thought I did a tremendous job in handling the situation. It was nice to hear, but nothing compared to the thanks and support I got from the residents. Coming from the people I'd helped, the thanks is of much more value and credibility.

My Own Brokenness—My Grieving Process

This design I created comes from my image, my emotions. This is my brokenness, my fear. Being recognized for what I did was never an expectation of mine. My focus and motivation were my residents. Maybe that's why my grieving process was . . . was . . . kind of warped . . . or delayed.

It differed from the normal grieving process because I wasn't simply focused on me. Being an RA delayed it. Those bursts of emotion that would smack me in the face, right before the memorial service, after my residents had left for Thanksgiving Break. That was my body saying, you're gonna deal with this on a personal level now. I couldn't stop and freeze the frame, and then go on, it's not reality. So I dealt with the situation. I was there for my residents. And I kept on doing what I usually did, schoolwork and classes. Life many times stinks this way. The world doesn't stop and wait for anyone.

I went home for Thanksgiving and was surrounded by relatives. When I spoke about what had happened, it was like telling strangers because I hadn't dealt with anything yet. And they weren't at school with me, living from day to day. I wanted them to simply be there, not ask questions and probe. They were a silent hug.

My family is of supreme significance to me. They play an important role in everything I do. Just talking to them on the phone was an opportunity for me to discuss my feelings and the events surrounding the death. They never asked specifically about it, but I always knew I could talk about it and they would listen. They would support me, reassure me, reaffirm me, and always be there.

Residents approached me to see how I was doing. I think they realized I had focused all my energy on them. I wasn't waiting

*for any of my residents to come up and ask how I was doing, but
it meant so much for them to ask. It was as if . . . I wasn't just
the RA, it was something beyond that, I was a person.*

Serving Up the Tray: Entering the Room Yourself
and Turning on the Light

*My finished design was in the shape of a circle. I wanted it to
be a full circle. I wanted the beer bottles to touch each other,
like holding hands. The six broken bottles form their community
with alcohol, the unbroken bottle, at the center. The design will
reach out to those who look at it, it will move you. Who is going
to get sucked into the circle next?*

*That's the purpose of the sixth bottle. The other five represent
students who died, but on the sixth, I put the words "Who's next?"
At the base of this sixth bottle are two broken bottle necks point-
ing at the person looking at it. As I imagine it, these broken pieces
form arrows. They point at whoever looks at the design and ask
the question "Who's next?" I wanted to make it personal for people so they wouldn't just see that it was sad. "Who's next?" This
bottle is just as much a part of the community as the other five
bottles.*

*At the base of the design is a newspaper headline written about
my school that appeared in the paper a couple of weeks after I
started the design. "No. 3 party school, again," Great, what does
that mean? It means that this place has great parties. But my
experience says we've had great loss too. My design is a combi-
nation of parties and losses.*

*I put this headline in my design because I feel like this is what
we're promoting. This kind of loss. This is what my university and
society are promoting with this kind of headline. For me, it promotes the image in my head that my design grew out of.*

*What about being a community? This university is seen as a
party school and from that we have to accept the consequences.
My image . . . this design . . . the consequences for us all.*

*I carried my design into class in a box. I wouldn't let anyone
see it, not even my professor. Originally, I figured I would just
put the design on a board or something. Oh, great. My friends
suggested that I go to a recycling place and find something, I
found a tray, a party tray for 25 cents. I polished it up so when
someone looked into it, they could see their reflection.*

I kind of served up my design on this party tray. This is really

*what I did when I showed it to the class. I served it up. It came
down from shoulder height and was placed in front of them.*

*When I served it up to them it looked very fresh, very real,
very much like it had just happened. The blood was real, but from
a package of liver. I wanted it to be a reflective thing for people,
kind of like seeing their reflection in the 25-cent polished tray.
When the light came down on it, it shined like it was in a party,
a party atmosphere. You had to look closely to see what was
really going on. It was like I was saying... my design was saying
. . . "okay deal with this. You have no choice but to deal with
this, like I had no choice."*

*If I had my choice when presenting it to the class, I would've
had them first see the design under a dim light, close to darkness, like the lighting at a party. Without preparing the audience,
have a bright light hit the design. The consequences of alcohol-
related deaths are what you see when the bright light hits the
design. I wanted to turn on the light for people about deaths related to alcohol. I wanted people to enter the room of anger, sadness, and depression that I entered. As a community, we are still
in the dim light. My design was my way of turning the bright
light on for the community. My hope is that people will turn this
bright light on for themselves and prevent themselves and others
from the consequences . . . becoming the sixth name appearing
on a shattered beer bottle within the circle, within the community
of alcohol-related deaths. Alcohol may not have been at the center of those students' lives but it was at the center of their deaths.
The sixth bottle . . .*

Who's next?

Who will be there to pick up the pieces?

Conclusion

As 45 per cent of traditional age college students continue to binge
drink one or more times in a two week period, the likelihood of this
scenario being repeated on college campuses is staggering. Using the
findings of this qualitative research study, a university community
can reevaluate protocols and responses to a student death. These tragedies receive attention and students receive support, yet do administrators prepare for what these students need six months or a year
after the death?

Another question resonating from the research is, how well do supervisors of resident assistants work with them during a tragedy? Focusing on the residents who are affected can become a consuming task. For the sake of these same residents, the resident assistant's expectations of him or herself must be kept in mind. It is essential to assess what responsibilities this student takes on, if these are appropriate responsibilities, and whether a solid rationale for these responsibilities exists.

Using this first hand account of a student's experience, the case study can be used with resident assistants in the following ways:

1. Read and discuss during an in-service training a couple of months into the semester;

2. Use as a reading assignment for a resident assistant class conducted during the semester;

3. Employ as a staff development topic during a staff meeting;

4. Encourage staff members to perform a one person play recounting the case study.

Administrators should read this case study reflecting on the struggle this resident assistant experienced in determining the administration's expectations of his role. The institutional expectations of a student in a helping role must be clearly articulated to ensure the student's mental, emotional, and physical well-being. Clear expectations further influence the well-being of the students these resident assistants encounter in their helping capacity. As administrators, what role do we allow these talented students to fill? Are these roles healthy and appropriate in such tragic circumstances?

The case study can be used with administrators in the following ways:

1. As a discussion tool to address the appropriate role of resident assistants in this type of situation.

2. As an evaluation protocol to ensure that supervisory concerns within the study are clearly understood.

3. As a means to conduct an organized discussion with administrators and resident assistants to examine mutual responsibilities and realistic expectations in an alcohol-related tragedy.

Student leaders can read this student's experience as a reflection upon the immense responsibility undertaken by them, often without warrant. They can use the case to determine realistic expectations for themselves as well as the appropriate helping role to fulfill during a student tragedy. This prior consideration may eliminate some of the pain and confusion that will undoubtedly occur if they choose to be *all* things to *all* their fellow students.

The case study can be used with student leaders in the following ways:

1. Student organizations can read and facilitate a discussion.

2. Student groups can evaluate the peer role they might play in an alcohol-related tragedy.

3. Individuals within student organizations can assess what services they might deem necessary for students experiencing this type of tragedy.

Summary

The reflections, perceptions, and experiences of this resident assistant provide a university community with an opportunity to gain a rich understanding of the expansive effects of an alcohol-related student death. This deeper understanding needs to permeate all aspects of an institution's response to such a crisis. University staff who react to a tragic situation without any previous training and preparation may further injure the individuals involved. Enacting strategies to prepare students and administrators to deal with these tragedies does not safeguard the community from pain and hurt, but may allow people to focus on addressing the tragedy, not on the effects of poorly constructed responses to a student death.

Most important, this research describes the tragic consequences of alcohol use which a university community fervently wishes did not occur. Yet, the chances of these tragedies occurring multiply significantly if students remain separated from the truth of the dangers of alcohol and their lives. Peer education bridges the gap between students' knowledge of alcohol and their lives. Peer education bridges the gap between students knowledge of alcohol and its tragic effects. This constructivist research case study links an effective university response to student tragedy and the reality that alcohol-related deaths persist.

References

Ely, M. with Anzul, M., Friedman, T., Garner, D., & Steinmetz, A.M. (1991). *Doing qualitative research: Circles within circles.* British, PA: Falmer Press.

Geertz, C. (1983). *Local knowledge.* New York, NY: Basic Books.

Glaser, B. D., & Strauss, A. K. (1967). *The discovery of grounded theory.* Chicago, IL: Aldine.

Guba, E., & Lincoln, Y. (1989). *Fourth generation evaluation.* Beverly Hills, CA: Sage.

Jenson, M. A., Peterson, T. L., Murphy, R.J., & Emmerling, D.A. (1992). Relationship of health behaviors to alcohol and cigarette use by college students. *Journal of College Student Development, 33,* 163–169.

Lincoln, Y., & Guba, E. (1985). *Naturalistic inquiry.* Beverly Hills, CA: Sage.

Lincoln, Y., Guba, E. (1986). But is it rigorous? Trustworthiness and authenticity in naturalistic evaluation. In D. Williams (Ed.), *Naturalistic evaluation: New Directions for Program Evaluation, No. 3,* (pp. 73–84). San Francisco, CA: Jossey-Bass.

Martin, C. M., & Hoffman, M. (1993). Alcohol expectancies, living environment, peer influence, and gender: A model for college-student drinking. *Journal of College Student Development, 34,* 206–311.

Presley, C. A., Mielman, P. W., & Lyerla, R. (1993). *Alcohol and drugs on American college campuses: Use, consequences, and perceptions of the campus environment* (Volume 1: 1989–1991). Carbondale, IL: Southern Illinois University, The CORE Institute, Student Health Program.

Shore, E. R., & Rivers, P. C. (1985). Peer pressure to drink: Implications for university administration and planning. *Journal of Alcohol and Drug Education, 30*(3), 22–31.

6

Respect and Dignity in the Free Marketplace of Ideas

Working Class Resistance within the University

Michael Paul Wong

Traditional visions of higher education have described this esteemed institution as one in which academic freedom is a transcendent virtue and every woman and man is accorded ample respect and dignity by one's peers. Ideally, the contributions of every person will be tested in the free marketplace of ideas for its validity (Bok, 1990; Boyer, 1987; Rosovsky, 1990; Smith, 1990). In the national consciousness of the United States, this vision addresses our highest goals of egalitarianism and the universal pursuit of truth. This notion of the university as a stage wherein people from disparate origins are able to encounter one another's views in an atmosphere of impartiality and collegiality has been a fundamental part of university culture in this country. It rises from the American university's elitist origins, and endures even to higher education's present-day turmoil over multiculturalism.

As a potential site for employment, this vision seems an exemplary place in which to "make a living." The ideal of the university offers the hope that, employed at these institutions, a modern citizen might balance contemporary society's virtual requirement that one put one's labor in the service of someone else with the particularly human need for individual autonomy and dignity. The siren call of this egalitarian free space of ideas is particularly compelling in a society of hierarchical divisions between classes (Aronowitz, 1983; Bowles & Gintis, 1976; Giroux, 1983), alienating relations between citizens and groups of citizens (Bellah, Madsen, Sullivan, Swidler, & Tipton, 1985; Boyer, 1987; Wineman, 1984), and meaningless consumption (Illich, 1970; Sennett & Cobb, 1972). For where else can we find meaning in the modern age if not in our work?

In the face of this ostensible congruence between self-image and livelihood, even a superficial inspection of the contemporary university often reveals not collegiality, but stratification. Instead, universities reflect, and perhaps even perpetuate, the unequal relationships of the larger society (Bowles & Gintis, 1976; Giroux, 1983; Smith, 1990). They are rarely places where members of a common community can face one another as intellectual equals on neutral ground.

My purpose in this rather indicting comparison of the ideal and the real is not to condemn the modern university. Rather, I submit that the university is the nexus of several uniquely American themes: the privileged and complex role of work in our society, the promise and ideal of educational opportunity as the "great equalizer," the role of education as a change agent in our society, and American society's egalitarian ideals. As both a workplace and a learning place, the university is a unique location to observe how Americans make meaning of both the contradictions and congruencies between the fundamental ideals of equality and liberty, and the reality of work in a segmented society.

Methodology

This research took place during a series of personal interviews with a university custodian over the course of a semester. These interviews took place "on the job," as Dee [a pseudonym], the respondent, went about her normal duties. There was little opportunity to observe Dee in interaction with others, because our interviews mainly took place after hours late at night.

Looking back on my case study, having written it, it must be evident that on many levels this was a personally difficult assignment for me. As the case study itself relates, my particular role as a first generation, Chinese Jamaican American son of working class immigrant parents made the topic of working class oppression a particularly emotional one for me. Furthermore, my father's experience as the possessor of a dominant class consciousness trapped by circumstances in a working class job contributed to my feelings of uneasiness with regard to this subject.

However, rather than attempt to get "distance" from these feelings, I attempted to explore them as much as possible, so that my particular experience would enrich rather than interfere with the research. My major dilemma once I got started with my research was how closely I should empathize with Dee. I was not so much concerned with "going native" (Geertz, 1983), as I was with allowing my personal voice and my very strong personal feelings in reaction to our subject matter to drown out Dee's voice. I tried to resolve this dilemma for myself in two ways. First, I decided that my personal and family background could inform this research, rather than overshadow it. Second, I worked to maintain the respondent's true words and voice as much as possible, while still telling a clear story throughout.

Although the oppressiveness of my personal baggage is felt by the reader in the ambivalence of the narrator's initial contact with Dee, as well as in the extended imagery of shadows and revealing light, I have overtly decided to make my personal contributions to this contact manifest in several ways. For one thing, my personal experience allows me to explore the emotional, as well as intellectual dimensions of Dee's story. Furthermore, I have found an ease at building a rapport or intimacy with the respondent (the reader might discern an apprehension, almost recoil, at this prospect in the case study, but ease is a developed, not automatic, state in any relationship). My personal experience with my respondent's frustrations, hopelessness, and meaning in spite of this situation helps me to empathize and celebrate her strength. Finally, it is almost impossible for me to intellectualize away Dee's feelings, which in my opinion results in a more honest, genuine and faithful study.

I attempted to resolve my fear of drowning out Dee's voice in another way by keeping my storytelling to her own words as much as possible. I tried to integrate anecdote and analysis in our study. In some places, my tentative conclusions are a bit muddier than others, but I feel that overall the story is authentic if not entirely linear and clear-cut. When I added words to her story for the sake of clarity, or reorganized her stories to reflect single topics, I worked to retain congruency between my dialogue and her monologue.

Toward the goal of authenticity, I submitted my writing and ideas to Dee for her agreement that I was accurately representing her understanding of our conversations. Member checking has been a simple affair for me, since Dee has very set working hours during which I can reach her, and because she is extremely interested in how this research turns out. Her enthusiasm is manifest at several points through the case study.

Some afterthoughts on the case study are that although Dee never explicitly mentioned it, at times I felt that she was overwhelmed by the idea that she was important enough to merit a full study. I questioned whether I was getting the full person, or the "public face." Were the answers I got a result of Dee being intimidated or conscious of the class differences between us?

Furthermore, I was concerned that my conclusions were becoming too literary or sentimental in my attempt to affirm the dignity of my respondent. Looking back on the written form of the case study, I have tried to present her as honestly as possible. I have intentionally avoided flowery description to avoid romanticizing Dee. I think that she would find sentimentality of her work silly and disrespectful. On the other hand, I really felt that I had to celebrate this woman's achievement at one point in the case study. I really felt that she was someone who has found meaning and self-worth in a field that society looks on as worthless or transitional.

In completing this study, I got the sense that I was taking part in the creation of fantasy world. The building transformed by the night into the custodian's private domain reminds me of the old myths from any culture in which the taken-for-granted everyday life is really a magical realm, but you need the magic eyes or glasses to be able to perceive it. Having done this study, I feel like I've put on these magical eyes for good.

As an anecdote, I've noticed that custodians seem to approach me more often in the past few months, and people who for me previously have been elements of the background have revealed themselves to my blindness as real human beings. This is not to congratulate myself, for it is truly I who have become more human in re-humanizing these people. Rather, I would just like to mention that with this study I feel like I have entered a fantasy world, and these human beings that I formerly took for granted as part of the scenery—furniture or walls—now take on life and brains and heart. In the same way, in the case study, the familiar surroundings of the building become new and frontier-like under Dee's guidance.

Finally, I felt that for me this was a process of coming to terms with my own feelings about my father and myself. This is not to seek some sort of written absolution for my lack of sensitivity as a child. However, to understand now is possible, and to celebrate another's sacrifice for the sake of a greater good is meaningful, and, I might say, heroic in itself.

I would have liked to do further exploration into Dee's sense of professionalism. From following my respondent through her daily work, I got such a sense of civic responsibility and the professional context and importance of her particular role in the university. Unfortunately, once I got to the writing stage of this project, I found that this sentiment, tacitly available in the field, was not reflected in what she had to say in my field notes. I would have liked to pursue this idea further, especially as it relates directly to the theme of finding meaning in a dehumanizing work environment, especially in light of Dee's particular place as a woman in this particular culture at this particular point in time and place.

Case Study: A University Custodian

There is darkness on the porch. One light shines above the door, resting upon the face of a woman standing alone, smoking a cigarette. For the moment I am as invisible as she feels, and I remain in the shadows to study her further. She seems peaceful, resting, but I can tell from here that this is a temporary state. She wears light clothing for the time of year, which is quite cold. Snow should be falling; it's cold, but the sky is black. Her features blend into the darkness of the night, the shadows making everything look unreal. I can see her breath mingle with the smoke from her cigarette until I can't really tell which is which in the cold evening night. She breathes quickly, which contradicts her seeming restfulness. She's wearing a light sweater and sweat pants. They're not particularly fancy clothes. They're not sloppy "work" clothes either. It's hard to see her eyes because of the glare from the porch's solitary light bulb on her glasses, so I move a bit closer. I'm not sure if she sees me, but I don't want to disturb her smoke. I approach quietly, almost gingerly. Up the steps (my weight makes the old wooden steps creak, which I did not notice in the blind rush of my customary approach) I climb, and she notices me. Ingenuous—I hope I look this genuinely glad to see her. I'm a little nervous; no, just cold. As we greet and exchange small talk—"how are you, what about this [new president] guy, have you met him"— I marvel how our breath intermingles in the cold of the night—it's hard to tell my breath and her smoke apart now as they both curlicue and spiral up out of the range of the light. There's a quiet moment as we both look out at the darkness. I can feel her respite; there's no putting off work to be done--her cigarette is almost finished. I feel cold, and I shiver just lightly. She notices and invites me in.

In the daytime this building is a bustling public administrative office. Tonight somehow I feel like I'm entering her home, or, more accurately, her private domain. Walking through empty offices, quiet hallways strangely lit with bright fluorescent bulbs yet absent of the normal hustle and bustle of normal office hours, the contrast between night and day is striking. I think of yin and yang—complementary opposites. She acts like a hostess showing off her home. "Here's P's office—you know him, right?" She gives me tours of "her" offices, showing off things that must be as familiar to her as they are to the people who inhabit the offices in the daytime. She gives me tours of offices that she knows I've worked in. There's almost an understanding that this building has somehow been transformed by the night, that the magic that allows me to see her as a visible human being will also allow me to see this old building as it truly is. It works.

In the brighter light of the indoor fluorescent bulbs, I can see her better. Her face shows an upbeat mood, alternating between cynicism and strong assertion, depending upon what she's talking about. She moves animatedly, moving from room to room as quickly as her train of thought moves from topic to topic, emptying trash, gesturing at the walls of a particularly clean or cluttered office. "This guy's really a slob. G's a good girl today; she didn't leave a mess for me." I'm noticing a kind of humming sound from the air or the lights; perhaps some machine left running late. It's quiet—almost lonely, except that we're not alone. "There's usually someone working late. I know people's schedules, and I know who's in at night." She rattles off people's schedules from memory.

It begins to occur to me that we are in the secret brain of the university. In the starkness of the cold, white office light, the vacant desks seem barren and naked, vulnerable to our eyes as we walk around them. Their secrets are all there to be perused, from the most confidential to the most trivial, if not today, then tomorrow. Here in this in-between world no door is closed. Every whisper is amplified

to a shriek, and the slightest scribble is magnified to great proportions. "I hear things no one on this campus hears. People leave their
memos or notes to their secretaries out on their desks all the time.
Guess who gets to read them? Oh, we hear all kinds of stuff. You
can get all kinds of dirt when you're a custodian." She grins at me,
wickedly:

> And not just from administrators. Who does security go to when
> they want the real news on what students are up to? The custodi
> ans! Oh yeah, I see the most interesting stuff out on these desks
> late at night sometimes. Or when I'm cleaning a building and there's
> a private meeting going on, they usually say, "Oh, it's just Dee. Go
> right ahead," and go right on talking about what they were talking
> about.

I wonder to myself how much confidential information this person has had knowledge of, as an almost literal fly on the wall at
these meetings, and, further, what it's like to have no effect whatsoever on the outcomes of these meetings. Is it powerful? Dehumanizing? I wonder most of all whether there is a difference between Dee's
voyeurism and my own as a researcher of another's life. Is there a
power in knowledge that is not encompassed in its use? Or is this
knowledge that is used?

> I don't repeat things that I see here. It's like a code of honor, that
> what I see and hear stays in here. I don't think that applies to ev
> eryone; it's just because I have ethics. There's no rule that says I
> can't talk about it. I just think that it would be wrong to use that
> information. You see, we see everything that goes on at this univer
> sity. Nothing happens that we don't see.

This line of thought gets me wondering— how important is it to
the system of authority at the university that custodians are kept quiet?
Why don't custodians get more involved in decision making, with
all of this inside information? "This doesn't mean I don't get involved in politics. That's how I get into trouble here sometimes."
She laughs easily, and leans back.

We are sitting together on a large couch in one of the office's
waiting areas. The wall opposite us is covered with flyers for vacations in the Caribbean, volunteer opportunities in Mexico, agricultural studies in Finland. We relax and chat for a while about her
daughter's plans to study in France as an exchange student,
while Dee smokes another cigarette. The room is slightly dark; the

light shines into it from the hallway area just enough to make a shadow of the entire room. The mood is intimate; the glow from the cigarette a warm orange in the shadows. I must confess that I'm thinking about warmer places than this New England university tonight.

> You know, we hear a lot of this university, but it's because nobody cares what we think. At this university, we're not important people, so they'll say whatever they want in front of us. That's why I'm so glad you're doing this research, because it's the first time anyone's asked. Nobody pays attention to me. It's like these professors. This academic office kept putting out bins of waste paper and not recycling, and I kept telling them that they would get fined $2,000 if they didn't start, but they didn't listen. So I reported the department, and they got in trouble. And you know what? The head of that department came and yelled at me! Well, I didn't have to take that, so I reported that professor to his department chair, and asked for an apology. That professor screamed and hollered at me for something I didn't even do, and what is it today— November 8—and they haven't done nothing. If nothing's done soon, I am going to take it to his dean. And if that doesn't work I will go straight to the president. I will go to Channel Three if I have to, and sit there until someone listens to me. If the university's crying now 'cause they ain't got no money, wait 'til I go to [the state capital]. That professor said I've got a big mouth, and that's right. Respect is important to me. Someone should know when one is right or wrong, and when one can prove it, someone should stand up from their rights. And if someone is wrong, they should be man or woman enough to admit it. That's what I teach my girls, and that's how I live my life. But this is what I've got to do to be heard.

She gets up again and moves into another room. Back to work. Dee continues:

> There's this professor on staff council, and he has an attitude that he's better than other people, and he doesn't like me. He presented this resolution before the staff council, and he wanted the council to single out his college. But I objected because the message was supposed to be unification; not special treatment. And you know what? The movement was defeated, mostly because of my objection. Well, he didn't like that, because I'm just a custodian. I'm not supposed to have this kind of influence. But, you know, everyone should be treated with respect. That's why I served on the

Respect Day Committee. When you get a college education you forget where you came from. You use big fancy words, Me, I'm just
plain and simple. If you keep it plain and simple, you have no problem.

I wondered whether the incident with the head of the department
would have been so intolerable had Dee been more respected as a
visible human being in her work. I also wondered whether the head
of the department would have found it as easy to yell at someone
who was not a university custodian. Our conversation moves to a
discussion of the latest student protest:

It's like when I talk with the kids at [the alternative university built
in protest of racial policies on campus]. Oh, I talk with those guys
all the time. They're a nice bunch of kids, although they're messy.
We talk about racism—real racism. I tell them you don't know anything about discrimination 'cause you come from an upper middle
class family in New York.

Given her experience with the problem, I have to see her point.
Dee is becoming less active. We seem to be nearing the end of
her workday. She takes more breaks, and pauses to speak more often
now. While she winds the cord of the vacuum cleaner around its
base, she explains to me the trick to get it to work properly,
because the cord is damaged. My assumption that her's is an easy
job is continually frustrated by the large amount of professional
knowledge required to complete her responsibilities. She glances at
her watch and announces suddenly that it's lunchtime. This gives me
a shock, since it's not even a round hour, must less noontime. Dee
assures me that this is the time that she takes a break for lunch
every day. I wonder aloud whether it really matters, because she
works alone. "If my manager walked in and caught me loafing around
she'd be a little upset, so I keep busy." I wonder what her manager
would think of someone following a custodian around asking questions about the quality of her work, or, more accurately, the meaning
that she finds it.

I love to talk to students. Oh, I'll sit all night with them at B Building sometimes. It's all a part of education, and, you know, whatever
I can do to further someone's education I'll do, because I think that's
so important. I think these kids can learn as much from me as from
these professors that give me such a hard time. Professors can learn
too, you know. Do you know B? He said to me, "I used to think

custodians were lazy, but now I think I need to look at them on
a one-to-one basis." S told me that she heard that he was very
insulting to custodians before—he made rude remarks when he
knew we could hear him. Now he's changed his opinion and
we have long conversations. We talk about Planning Council; all
kinds of things. He's got a new respect for custodians, mainly because of me.

It's the same thing with Staff Council. Some of these administrators have been administrators so long they've forgotten who they
are. They need to learn that everyone deserves respect— including
custodians. People need to listen to one another. I really think that
I would get more involved if management would let me, but it scares
them for me to get involved and make connections with people above
their heads and share information with students.

She gazes out of the window. Her meal finished, she pulls out a
cigarette and lights it. We're standing on opposite sides of the room
now, leaning against the walls. For all the hustle of her evening, I
feel like I'm more winded trying to keep up with her. All is silent
in the building, and it's almost a relief to see an everyday world
going on outside through the window. The headlights of a few cars
light up as they pull out of the parking lot. Other custodians going
home for the evening? We quickly walk back through each office
for a quick check; then she carefully locks the door of each office
and we proceed back to the couch. She's relaxed again, peaceful as
before. "Among the custodians we have an unwritten rule on Friday.
We don't bust our butts for nobody." We both laugh, the sound seeming almost irreverent in the waiting quietness of the empty building.
We sit in the shadows and chat together. Dee pulls out another cigarette and lights it.

"Yeah, management doesn't like us fraternizing too much with
the folks in my buildings. As soon as I start getting friendly with
the people there, and they start giving me letters of recommendation, management gets mad and pulls me." "Oh"—she brightens up.
"I got a letter of recommendation from L. Letters piss my supervisor
off." She grins at me.

Remember when I used to work in B Building? There were lots of
students there all the time. I had more personal contacts, my sick
time went down, I missed less days, and they loved me there. I had
the personality to match the building. When I agreed to sit on the
search committee for the new building manager, I got pulled. The

bosses don't like us getting too close to the people.

They pulled me out of S Building the same way. There was no communication or discussion about it. They said that the office people complained that menial tasks were being done from two to four. But, Mike, if they were so unhappy with my work, why did they write me letters thanking me for this and that? M thinks I'm a threat because I'm popular with the administration. I think it's a personal problem between me and her. I think she doesn't like that I take center stage when we're in a room together. As soon as I start getting popular with the people in a building and getting letters of recommendation management pulls us.

I'm starting to feel uncomfortable. I have no intellectual understanding of management-labor relations, but it's a raw subject for me. I tell her about my father. My father came to this country from a wealthy background in his own country. He was educated and cultured, but he came to this country with almost nothing. To survive, he took on a job as a supermarket clerk. He did this for the sake of the family, and for the sake of the family he remained a supermarket clerk for the next 30 years, until he felt that he was too old to change careers. When Dee speaks of her impotency and frustration with management, she begins to sound very much like my father. I'm beginning to think that I originally chose Dee as a subject because of my family's pseudo-working class background, and my memories of my father's frustrations on the job. The discomfort increases as our discussions stir up painful memories from my childhood. Her complaints about harassment on the job—both overt and hidden—from "management types" are disturbingly similar to those that my father used to bring home after late nights on the job at the supermarket. Being a kid, I was more embarrassed that my father worked at the supermarket than sympathetic toward the frustrated human being who had to go there night after night. As I leaned back in the couch with Dee, I wondered how it is that I had to go 4,000 miles away to come to terms with my own father.

My father also saw through his management. He understood when the bosses were trying to force him to quit, and when they would suddenly give him whatever he asked for to gain his leadership on a labor issue. But he never got involved to the extent that Dee has, because he never intended to stay as long as he did. What does it feel like to have one's hopes and ambitions confined to this building's nighttime hours, or a supermarket register?

Dee continues:

> The only good manager was R, and now he's no longer a manager.
> He treated us custodians like people. He grew up here and he knows
> us. You won't find one custodian who trusts management. Manage-
> ment doesn't like it when you get along with people above them.
> These people rely on what I call "intimidation management." You
> count on them for a job, so you let them treat you any way they
> want. This is how management feels. But you know, there's such a
> thing as freedom of speech in this country. Anyway, the worst thing
> that they can do is fire me. I came here in the middle of January in
> a snowstorm. It's winter again, and I can leave. I may just be a
> custodian on the staff council, but I see things.

Looking at her now, I see so much more than a role, or a part of
the scenery. Sitting together in the profound stillness of the empty
building, I have to marvel how Dee has maintained her humanity in
spite of her working conditions. In response to her management's
arbitrary exercise of authority, she asserts the solidarity among staff
members and students: "everyone should be treated with respect; that's
what this is all about." In response to confidential information, she
creates a code of honor in the sharing and use of that information:
"it's just because I have ethics: if someone is wrong they should be
man or woman enough to admit it." In response to invisibility, she
responds with self-assertion. I exist! I think, and act and feel! "And
if they won't hear me, I'll sit on the steps of the television station
until someone talks to me."

Implications

A primary theme pervading this study was the exploration of authority and the exercise thereof. I saw the higher education institution
in its roles of both school and workplace as a place where ideas
of authority and power were constantly being re-interpreted and
acted out. This issue is present in the literature on education in a
capitalist society. From this perspective, education could be seen as
a place where authority was granted through accreditation and ap-
proval (to the students, and to the managers), and where authority
was exercised and challenged (by the managers and by the workers,
respectively).

In this particular case, the school becomes a double site of resistance, as student and worker come together to compare their perceptions of authority and the domination of authority. To Dee, the university is a site of struggle, a place where one does not just earn a living, but also a place where one must defend one's self-dignity and humanity against the arbitrary abuse of power by those who have it. It is a place where untouchable bureaucrats exercise "intimidation management" because they know that you need the job.

On the other hand, the workplace is a site of often playful resistance. As an ostensibly "free marketplace of ideas," the university has built in several avenues in which workers can affect the institution, such as the Staff Council and the various committees on which Dee sits. Dee is quite proud of her exercise of power, often mentioning the marks that she has personally made on the quality of life here. These marks range from her interactions with students, staff, and faculty, to her role in the Staff Council as a "troublemaker" who safeguards her sense of justice.

Violence seems to be a creeping theme, not so much in the overt sense, but as an ever-present threat should one step out of one's place in the dominant structure. Dee takes full advantage of the power guaranteed her in American institutions (note her threat to use the media and her personal relationships with high-level administrators). This is when force plays out in her life. Particularly critical is the tension she negotiates between non-personhood in silence, and the exercise of violence against her by authorities once she speaks up. Although her material existence is not threatened by these authorities, she feels a definite threat of violence from professors who feel free to treat her with hostility, and from administrators whose authority is threatened by her dominance at Staff Council meetings. Certainly, the constant changing of work environment and hours threatens her role as a mother to her two daughters.

Information and its uses also appears as a theme in our conversations. Although never articulated in her job description, Dee prides herself on her integrity. This integrity plays out in a code of honor that proscribes sharing of what she sees and hears on the job. It is interesting to me that she refuses to use this potential source of power "because I've got morals," regardless of the poor treatment that she receives from her superiors. On the contrary, Dee expresses a collegial concern for the inhabitants of "her" buildings, often locking cabinets left unlocked and replacing misplaced items.

This concern for others, what I see as an integration of caring and professionalism, seems to infuse meaning into her work through her interactions with others, and through networking with students, faculty, and administrators. In the midst of what Illich (1970) would probably see as meaningless work in the service of equally meaningless consumerism seems to dwell hints of his "emergent minority," the end result of the banishment of the consumer state, that "loves people more than products" and "values hope above expectation" (p. 165).

In response to the arbitrary exercise of power and its abuse, Dee gains a feeling of superiority through her strong sense of civic responsibility. Dee adamantly sticks to personal truths ("everyone is equal and has a right to be heard"), even when they are at odds with the dominant ideology. It is interesting that Sennett and Cobb (1972) tie workers' sense of inadequacy to the perception of having a poor mind or lack of intelligence, for Dee feels superior to faculty and administrators. She feels equal mentally, and morally superior. She "sees through their schemes," and sees herself in the role of whistle blower, who is able to interpret to others what's "really going on up there in administration." We see this in her experiences of reciprocal learning and solidarity with student groups, as she draws connections between their mutual lack of formal authority.

What little personal power she has on the job Dee sacrifices in order to remain true to her personal sense of morality. Although the supervisor who mistreats her is not watching her at every moment, she strictly works her hours to the minute. Furthermore, as a single mother, who works the late shift because she has to, she refuses to work weekends, even though it promises a more affluent lifestyle or threatens her job, because working weekends means missing out on her daughters' childhood. The sacrifice of power for the ones one loves is a theme in much of the ethnographic literature (Sennett & Cobb, 1972). In relation to this sacrifice, Sennett and Cobb write of a father sacrificing to gain the feeling that he is "building some meaning, that he is adding something to the world in which he was born" (p. 134). However, in Dee's case, one does not feel the sense of despair and desperation evoked by these authors. Rather, I felt that her sacrifice is a just price to pay for the enjoyment of her daughters' company.

In conclusion, my conversations with Dee reveal that for her, the workplace and the institution are much more than just a site of struggle or indoctrination. Her work is also a site of responsibilities, caring, and sacrifice. Likewise, Dee's work as a university custodian is more than just a role of subordination to the arbitrary exercise of authority and violence. It can also be the site of resistance, and the exercise of power on the margins of the dominant system. However, in the same way, the university's role as an ideological free space has its inherent contradictions in light of its simultaneous place as a site of working class struggle against dominant class authority and the dehumanization of the greater class structure. This struggle can be playful, as in Dee's "troublemaker" role on the Staff Council, or it can be serious, as in her relationship with her supervisor.

Can the workplace be a field of resistance, even more so within the ideological "free market of ideas" of the ostensibly egalitarian university? Can this "free market" contain the silencing and dehumanization that takes place in the background of the university? If nothing else, the contradictions indigenous to this institution can be seen in its multiple roles as workplace and marketplace.

References

Aronowitz, S. (1983). *Working class hero.* New York, NY: Pilgrim.

Bellah, R. N., Madsen, R., Sullivan, W. M., Swidler, A., & Tipton, S.M. (1985). *Habits of the Heart: Individualism and commitment in American life.* New York, NY: Harper and Row.

Bok, D. (1990, May-June). What's wrong with our universities? *Harvard Magazine,* 44–59.

Bowles, S., & Gintis, H. (1976). *Schooling in capitalist America.* New York, NY: Basic Books.

Boyer, E. (1987). *College.* New York, NY: Harper and Row.

Dill, D. D. (1991). The management of academic culture: Notes on the management of meaning and social integration. In M. W. Peterson (Ed.), *Organization and governance in higher education* (pp. 182–194). Needham Heights, MA: Ginn.

Geertz, C. (1983). "From the native's point of view": On the nature of anthropological understanding. In C. Geertz (Ed.), *Local knowledge* (pp. 55–70). NY: Basic Books.

Giroux, H. (1983). Theories of reproduction and resistance in the new sociology of education: A critical analysis. *Harvard Educational Review, 53*(2), 257–293.

Illich, I. (1970). *Deschooling society.* New York, NY: Harper Colophon.

Rosovsky, H. (1990). *The University*. New York, NY: Norton.

Sennett, R., & Cobb, J. (1972). *The hidden injuries of class*. New York, NY: Vintage.

Smith, P. (1990). *Killing the spirit*. New York, NY: Viking.

Wineman, S. (1984). *The politics of human services*. Boston, MA: South End Press.

7

Footsteps of Courage

A Case Study of Felice

Jennifer Hart

As an adult daughter of an alcoholic father, I continue to explore my own past. Through my exploration, I realized how important it was to find meaning in my experiences as well as in the story of another adult daughter of an alcoholic father. Sharing the story of another would help me pursue and further articulate my assumptions, so central to constructivist inquiry. Also, I felt that my perspective growing up in an alcoholic home would assist me in seeing things that others might not be able to see.

Since I am an adult daughter of an alcoholic living on a college campus and have attended campus adult children of alcoholics (ACOA) support groups, I did not want to choose a respondent with whom there was a potential for dual roles. Therefore, I asked a colleague at a nearby college to serve as my gatekeeper. In her gatekeeper role, I also hoped that she would begin to set the foundation for a trusting relationship with my respondent. She introduced me to Felice [a pseudonym], marking the beginning of our journey together.

Literature Review

Estimates suggest that there are between 28 and 34 million adult children of alcoholics in the United States (Black, 1981; Black, 1990; Goodman, 1987; Kinosian, 1987; Rearden & Markwell, 1989). Many of these ACOAs are traditional-aged college women. Despite the numbers of adult women who grew up in alcoholic families, there is inadequate literature that focuses solely on the experience of females. The research centers primarily on the population of male adult children (Ackerman, 1989; Benson & Heller, 1987; Berkowitz & Perkins, 1988; El-Guebaly & Offord, 1977; Guinta, 1992; Levenson, Oyama, & Meek, 1987). Certainly some of the experiences of ACOAs are common to both genders, but differences do exist (Levenson, et al.). Similarly, as students move through college, male and females encounter many of the same developmental challenges; but as Belenky, Clinchy, Goldberger, and Tarule (1986) and Josselson (1987) contended, women are likely to experience their identity development differently than men. Thus, it is important to examine the experiences of adult daughters of alcoholics, especially as they matriculate through college and continue to develop their sense of self.

As children, many such daughters live in a system fraught with denial; they become survivors (Ackerman, 1989; Black, 1981; Black, 1990; Brown, 1988; Friel & Friel, 1988; Seixas & Youcha, 1985; Woititz, 1983). As adults, they struggle with self-definition and identity development (Ackerman; Brown; Downing & Walker, 1987; Filstead, McElfresh, & Anderson, 1981; Goodman, 1987; May & Maniacek, 1987). Although some adult daughters face challenges, due in part to their childhoods, their development need not stagnate. Healing and growth can and does occur in their lives (Ackerman; Brown; Cermak, 1988; Friel & Friel; Kinosian, 1987; May & Maniacek; Seixas & Youcha; Woititz). The following review of the literature traces some childhood patterns of adult children and focuses specifically on denial, survival, identity development, and recovery for adult women.

Denial

Denial can serve a healthy purpose, depending on how it is used. When individuals suffer a crisis or loss, denial protects them until they are ready to face the reality of what happened. In an alcoholic family, the crisis that children face is constant. Denial becomes a way of life rather than a protective mechanism used only when necessary (Friel & Friel, 1988).

The primary role of denial in an alcoholic family is to keep the status quo. Denial serves to keep the family secret of alcoholism (Brown, 1988; Seixas & Youcha, 1985). Even within the family, the truth about the disease is rarely discussed (Woititz, 1983). Denial becomes so pervasive that the family (including the children) becomes increasingly isolated. In order to maintain the secrecy, it is necessary for family members to withdraw from others (Brown). In fact, Brown contended that the role of denial is often so all-encompassing that it becomes the only sense of self that children in the family develop. As children create their self-image, they exclude a range of emotional experiences to be consistent with the secrecy of the family story—they deny themselves (Black, 1990; Brown).

Adult children are survivors of a double bind: they are afraid to move beyond the secrecy and talk about the alcoholism; remaining alone, they continue to strengthen the denial by not talking (Seixas & Youcha, 1985). Denial becomes a significant foe in the ACOAs' search for themselves (Woititz, 1983). Denying the alcoholism and themselves are challenges that adult daughters must confront to move toward personal growth and self-awareness (Woititz).

Surviving in the Family System

Children growing up in alcoholic homes often learn roles (like denial) based on their perception of what they need to do to survive and to bring stability to their lives (Ackerman, 1989; Black, 1981; Cermak, 1988; Gravitz & Bowden, 1985; Rearden & Markwell, 1989). Unpredictability characterizes alcoholic families and children become reactors to the family crisis of alcoholism (Black). These children shut down their emotional lives so that the feelings of fear, anger, pain, and abandonment cannot overwhelm them (Gravitz & Bowden). They become codependents in order to survive (Black, 1990; Fischer, Spann, & Crawford, 1991).

Fischer, Spann, and Crawford (1991) defined codependency as

a psychosocial condition that is manifested through a dysfunctional pattern of relating to others. This pattern is characterized by: extreme focus outside of self, lack of open expression of feelings, and attempts to derive a sense of purpose through relationships. (p. 88)

Children in alcoholic families often develop the characteristics of codependency in order to protect themselves, to be able to function despite the chaos created by the alcoholism. Research suggests that codependency and femininity are positively related (Fischer et al, 1991); daughters of alcoholics are more likely to exhibit codependent behaviors than sons.

As children grow up and leave the alcoholic family, some of them maintain their survival skills, as if they are second-nature (Ackerman, 1989; Black, 1990; Gravitz & Bowden, 1985). Unfortunately, some of those skills that once served to meet the expectations of others and create balance are no longer functional for ACOAs as they begin to live without the constant crisis of alcoholism (Ackerman; Cermak, 1988). Another problem that many ACOAs face as they continue to manifest codependent behaviors is that they lose their sense of self; the codependency becomes a mask for them and from others (Ackerman).

Identity Development

As adult children, denial and other survival behaviors continue to be central. The literature suggests that maintaining these characteristics as adults overshadows personal growth and identity development (Ackerman, 1989; Brown, 1988; Downing & Walker, 1987; Filstead, et al, 1981; Goodman, 1987; May & Maniacek, 1987). Young adulthood marks the time in the lives of many individuals when identity formation takes precedence (Ackerman, 1989; Brown, 1988; Chickering, 1969; Gilligan, 1982). For many adult children, these seemingly "normal" developmental challenges seem more difficult as these young adults carry the coping patterns learned as children (Ackerman; Downing & Walker, 1987; Filstead et al, 1981; Goodman, 1987).

For many women, identity development is achieved through connectedness rather than separation (Belenky et al, 1986; Gilligan, 1982; Josselson, 1987). This desire for relational communion intensifies the challenges that many adult daughters face as they seek to discover their sense of self. This process is especially significant since separation and isolation are behaviors that have become second nature for them (Ackerman, 1989). Identity, for these codependents, is fused with their roles in the preservation of the family system. They cannot be themselves unless they are acting out their family roles, even if they are no longer living in the family system (May & Maniacek,

1987). Adult daughters can feel caught between two different worlds. They feel pulled by a loyalty to the family, maintained by denial, and they feel an equal pull toward finding themselves through experiences with others (Ackerman; Brown, 1988).

Recovery

Despite the challenges that many adult daughters face in their identity development due in part to denial and other survival roles, personal growth is not impossible. The process of recovery includes breaking down the barriers that were created to survive in the family system (Kinosian, 1987). Recovery, like identity formation for many women, is a process that cannot be accomplished alone (Friel & Friel, 1988). For, as these authors claimed, isolation serves to protect denial and it is through exposing and admitting the denial that adult daughters, in particular, can find themselves.

Recovery involves converting survival skills into growing skills (Ackerman, 1989). Some of the skills adult daughters learn can be substantial assets (Ackerman; Benson & Heller, 1987; Clair & Genest, 1987; Gravitz & Bowden, 1985). For example, Ackerman suggested that many adult daughters learned how to survive, handle crises, take care of themselves, and be dependable. These skills were invaluable for adult daughters as children and will continue to assist them as adults.

While positive life skills should be utilized and treasured, it is important that adult daughters also give up their unhealthy, codependent self (Ackerman, 1989). He defined recovery as "a gift of self" (p. 1982). This means that adult daughters need to understand, accept, and work through their childhood. Recovery allows these women to go beyond their childhood experiences and become the adult they would like to be (Ackerman; Black, 1981; Black, 1990; Kinosian, 1982). Neither recovery nor discovering and developing a healthy self are destinations, rather they are continuous processes. The heart of these growth processes is liking themselves and becoming the women that they would like to be.

Methodology

My gatekeeper (Lincoln & Guba, 1985) helped me establish initial trust with Felice, but I was concerned that she would still be hesitant to share some of her more difficult experiences with me. I explained to Felice that I was an adult daughter of an alcoholic myself, and that helped to strengthen the trust even more. Also, her own healing and strength contributed to her willingness to share her story not only with me, but with all those who read this case study.

Date collection took place over multiple formal interviews. During our first meeting, we co-constructed a consent form that outlined the possible uses for the research, assured her anonymity, and explained the commitment we were making in pursuing this project. Felice was not concerned about her own anonymity and wanted to use her own name, reflective of her strength and comfort of self. Despite her request, I explained the significance of anonymity in this research design (Lincoln & Guba, 1985) and she then chose to name herself "Felice."

I took notes during our interviews, trying to identify key words and phrases, later typed them up into field notes, and returned those notes to Felice to be member checked (Lincoln & Guba, 1986; Manning, 1997). These notes included my interpretations of her experiences and an attempt to reflect the meaning of what she had shared. Felice commented both on the accuracy of her story and on my interpretations throughout the process.

One of the most rewarding moments for me during the member checking process came in a letter Felice sent to me. In her letter, she referred to an interpretation I had made about some of the relationships she had before coming to college. She thanked me for helping her see her experience in a way that she had not considered, finding new meaning in her own story.

By the end of the third interview, I notice that patterns and themes were consistently emerging (Lincoln & Guba, 1985). Also, the data began to repeat themselves, indicating that I could put closure to our guided conversations.

The data I collected were powerful and rich. Selecting the most salient themes was a challenge; but with Felice's assistance, we were able to choose themes that were most meaningful. As those themes developed into working hypotheses, I was able to begin writing a draft of the case study.

It was important to me to convey Felice's voice, so I decided to work with her to tell her story in the first person. My interpretations would remain in the third person in order to make a distinction between her meaning and assumptions and mine. I completed two drafts, giving each to Felice for her feedback and changes when necessary.

I also included an audit trail within the context of our case study so that the data could be traced back to the field notes.

As I read and reread the case study, I found that I had become too close to the data and could not adequately assess whether or not the story made sense. Additionally, I felt that my experiences resulted in taking some language for granted, making it difficult for other readers to make their own interpretations. In order for me to regain perspective, members of my peer debriefing group (Ely, Anzul, Freidman, Garner, & Steinmetz, 1991; Lincoln & Guba, 1985) read and critiqued the initial draft.

Through the use of internal and external audits, I was able to complete a final draft of the case study that shared the footsteps of Felice's journey, the journey of an adult daughter of an alcoholic father. For Felice and me, the consistent search for meaning and deep reflection was a rewarding process. Through it, an important perspective is revealed that is influenced, but not determined, by growing up in an alcoholic home.

Case Study

Growing up as an adult daughter of an alcoholic father is a journey of healing, filled with courage. Felice, a senior at a small religiously-affiliated college in New England, shares a rich story, one that is difficult to tell, about her experiences growing up as a daughter of an alcoholic father.

Her journey is not on a rocky road nor on a smooth glass surface. Felice begins to lead us on a path that meanders through sunny meadows and overcast valleys. She shares her footsteps of courage, trust, control, and a childhood lost. At times, the path becomes muddied and it may be difficult to distinguish particular steps. But, the footsteps, whether crisp or coupled, mark her journey.

Felice takes many steps forward. Growing up, her forward steps were often survival techniques and protection mechanisms that were independent and brave. Now, her steps forward include other people; her steps are interdependent with others, and have contributed to her healing. This connection for which she longed seems to fill a void. But, it is not until her journey brings her to college that she begins to focus on and tries to fill that emptiness. The bravery in her new steps comes from taking risks that were unsafe in her family.

Taking risks is not always easy nor successful for Felice. She sometimes takes steps backward when she confronts challenges that are too difficult to overcome. Yet, Felice recognizes her struggles and understands that she may need to step backwards to one day move forward.

Felice has grown and discovered herself throughout her journey, and as her journey continues beyond the context of these next pages, so will her growth.

Footsteps of Courage

My father is the alcoholic in my family. I knew about his alcoholism, and like the rest of my family, kept the "family secret." But, I didn't look at growing up in an alcoholic home until I could really focus on myself. I went to some ALANON meetings (i.e., support groups for friends and family members coping with alcoholism) with my mother while in high school, but until the focus was only on me and I was on my own, I didn't really look at it.

When I was a freshman, I was at a point in my life when I just needed someone to listen. I was fortunate to meet Ann, the director of freshman programs, when I did. She listened to me. She also acknowledged that what I went through was hell. I needed to hear that. She also helped me see that there were some positive aspects to all my struggles.

When Ann recognized that I wanted to work on things, she referred me to Holly, a counselor on campus. I met with her individually a few times and she told me that she was forming a group for Adult Children of Alcoholics. I decided to join the group and continue to meet with Holly individually.

Ann and Holly encouraged me to share my experiences with other people. I've done programs for first year students about my experiences growing up with an alcoholic father. But, I don't think that I would be as comfortable sharing my experiences if I hadn't started by sharing my stories with my ACOA group.

The group was good, really good. I used to think that everyone is fighting a battle. The group helped me see that my battle was real. I also learned that I was not alone. I was not the only one with struggles, struggles that I wanted to work on. I learned to turn it around. If I don't resolve my past, I can't live in the present and the future.

I still have difficulties with things from my past, not everything is resolved. There is still a hesitation, a feeling of being uncomfortable, when I talk about my father, especially in the context of the past. Like I've said, I've come a long way, but I still have a long way to go.

Footsteps of Trust

It is really hard for me to trust. It is hard to open up to others about who I am. It is not easy to let people be my friends. I'm afraid of being abandoned. Part of this difficulty in trusting came from growing up in an alcoholic home.

In living with my father, I become afraid to put my guard down. I learned that walking on egg shells was the way to live. I was afraid that if I would open up, someone wouldn't like me. I just wasn't confident with myself. I didn't trust that others would like me, and I couldn't trust that I liked myself.

My father, who I thought I was supposed to trust, set the stage for me not trusting others. I'd sometimes wonder, did the alcohol make my father loud and obnoxious, or is he that way without it? I don't know him. I never had the opportunity to know him, let alone trust him and his unpredictability. The fear of unpredictability kept me from being able to talk to him and create a trusting relationship.

This lack of trust led to internal and external pressures to do well. In part, overachieving became a survival technique because no one else was going to be there to count on—I had to do the work of two people. I had to push myself. But, I'm beginning to work on this perfectionist drive, and learning to trust myself and others.

Trusting myself took a long time. It wasn't until I was in college that I took the first step. I have learned the hard way. Life has not been a bed of roses and sometimes I've been burned. But I've learned to take risks. They may be baby steps, but I'm bridging gaps. Being affirmed has helped me take those initial steps in trust. Ann, Holly, the group, and my mother have helped by affirming who I was. Affirmation began to help me see that I was okay, and thus I could open myself up.

Trust goes beyond myself and others. The idea of serenity is linked closely to trust. Serenity means that I am at peace with myself. I trust my Higher Power that wherever I am and whomever I am with is right for me at that time in my life. Serenity means

*having trust that I have faith to let go, others are the way they
are and I cannot change that. I have the ability to love myself.*

Footsteps of Intimacy

*Growing up, I was superwoman. The teachers loved me because
I was involved and spent a lot of time on academics. But, I was
lonely because the kids saw me as a good student. I just wanted
to be accepted. I was the girl who could do everything. I was
sixth in my class, the president of the National Honor Society,
president of my class. I did all these things. But, rather than getting closer to others through these activities, it put distance between me and others. Social activities required too much intimacy.
So, inside I was very lonely.*

*Being a superwoman was also part of my perfectionist streak.
This meant that everything had to be just right. I couldn't rock
the boat or take a risk that someone would not like me, so I didn't
let anyone get close. Rocking the boat meant that my father would
have a tantrum, so I kept to myself.*

*The connection that did exist in my childhood was with my fam-
ily. The connection in growing up is that blood is thicker than
water. This means keeping the family secret—what happens in the
house, stays in the house. Living the family secret kept us together and let no one else in. It became our mission to keep the family secret. Inside the house, it was gloom and doom, but there
was a picket fence and a perfect daughter on the outside. That
was the way that I lived, connected to the family and the secret
on the inside and isolated from everyone on the outside.*

*I carry on many of the messages I learned at home, but many
of them changed as I changed and developed. Intimacy has grown
to be a big thing for me. Intimacy was once based on immediate
physical gratification, but I soon realized that wasn't cool. I began to reassess my definition of intimacy.*

*Intimacy with others became emotional, getting to know an-
other person. It was not necessarily sexual or physical. I was able
to explore ways to become close that at one time I never considered intimate.*

*I am affirmed by my connection with women. This connection
became real to me when I came to college. The group was all
women and there was a camaraderie among us. The group was
one of the places that I felt associated as a woman. I now have
an incredible feeling of power and control being a woman. I feel*

an emotional connection with women, and being intimate with both men and women. It has become trust, letting another person in my life. It has become understanding what others go through as a person.

Footsteps of Control

The unpredictability of my family, particularly my father, contributed to my difficulty in trusting others. It also equated to chaos, and a lack of control. I never knew if my father would be roaring drunk or passive. I never brought anyone home because I couldn't predict or control the situation and I certainly couldn't let them in on the family secret. From Friday night through the end of the weekend, we lived in fear, fear of unpredictability.

This fear went beyond the house too. At parent-teacher conferences, he would make wise-cracks and be loud. He would just be a jerk, saying things completely out of the blue. I would get embarrassed and be on the edge of my seat worrying about what he might say or do. I remember being ten years old and having to worry how my father would be when he would come to pick me up from school. Would he be drunk? If he was, would he be loud and obnoxious, or would he be quiet and passive? It makes me sick to my stomach to even think about that now.

I never knew what to expect from my father, except chaos. I felt completely out of control, especially when he was violent. As a matter of fact, there is still a hole in our kitchen wall that serves as a reminder of that violence and uncontrollable rage. The hole is there from a fight I had with my father. He threw me into the wall.

Reliving the violence and the very traumatic memories are hard. There was a great deal of physical abuse related to the alcohol, a lot of it directed at me. I saw it so often, that I thought the abuse was a way of communicating. Violence was role modeled by my father. And, you model your role model.

One day, my mother was in the living room on the couch. My father had just gotten out of the shower. There was another argument, I don't really know what it was about. My father was drunk and he was annoying me. I felt myself getting so angry. He enraged me so much and I internalized most of it. But I couldn't keep it in any longer. So, I went into the dining room and picked up a heavy oak dining room chair. I swung it on his body.

He said, "Go ahead, hit me some more." This just made me more angry. I fell to the floor and cried.

I said, "I want to die, I don't want to live anymore."

My mother just sat and watched me. She did nothing. I felt betrayed by my mother. I just wanted to end it all. At the time, I didn't understand why she didn't do anything. But, that's when my mother was really sick. We all were. The disease wasn't just my father's.

Sometimes, I wish he'd hurt me physically so someone would see what was going on. It was a warped sense of reality. I wanted to be hospitalized or to end it all. I kept trying to find ways to gain some control of the situation, but I couldn't.

Control is a big issue. My father always wants to be in control, and in some ways, so do I. I wanted control of the chaos, the unpredictability, the violence, but I couldn't get it. Instead, I found other ways to be controlled. Anger was a control. Also, I was very self-disciplined and self-motivated. Basically, all things equaled control. My perfectionist streak is a control issue, yet I don't really have control of that. Being a perfectionist means that I'm never going to be good enough.

I've learned that setting limits is a much healthier way to have control. It is self-control, not externally motivated. I have tried to set some boundaries with my father. My father calls a lot, especially when things are not going well for him. Sometimes, I feel sorry for him, and I find myself getting sucked in. What I realized is that I have to keep trying to re-establish boundaries and it may mean taking a risk. It is a risk to have boundaries, but I am learning to take those risks.

It takes time to relax and let go. I've learned to focus on myself and not my father. He's the alcoholic, but I am the codependent and the ACOA. My home life has developed into the person that I am. Now, I have the power to be what I want to be. I can make my own choices and decisions. But, it is not so controlled that I can't let others in. I can now let others have influences on me, and I can set boundaries when I am not ready for those influences.

Footsteps of a Childhood Lost

In the things that I did around the house, I felt like I was ten going on 30. I had a lot of chores growing up. I did things that were not expected of a child at an early age. I did the laundry, dishes, took out the garbage, and took care of my brother. I had to do these things because not doing them meant rocking the boat. I sadly admit that I had no childhood.

I felt like I was the mother in my family. I don't know if my mother would agree, for she wouldn't want to lose her motherhood. But, I took care of my brother a lot, and even now, I look out for his safety. It is not just being a mother to my brother though. Sometimes I was a mother to my parents. I was protective and concerned for everyone's well-being.

Not only was it reinforced to do "motherly" things, but even doing "childlike" things was negatively reinforced. I remember one night, my father asked me to pick up my toys. I didn't respond to his request. So, he picked up a bag, put all my toys in it, and threw them away. I learned that messiness was not acceptable. Instead, I become a perfectionist, making sure everything was just the way it was supposed to be.

I do miss my childhood. I lost a lot of it, but it wasn't all bad. My mother took time, she was there for us. She was the kind of mom who was baking cookies when we got home from school. She was the field trip mother, the mother who went to parent-teacher conferences. So, I did have a childhood with my mother and brother. But I consider a family with a father, and he wasn't there. That's where the childhood got lost.

My life can be broken down into three time periods: the time when the dysfunction was most present, when my mother and father were married; the time when it was my mother, my brother and me; and the recent present, since my mother remarried. When there was just my mother, brother, and me that was the happiest time for me. This feeling of loss is like a death in my life. I am never going to be able to experience my life as it was before because of my mother's new marriage.

Implications and Recommendations

In many ways, the literature complements and parallels Felice's journey. Her story is one of self and recovery. Through her footsteps of courage, trust, and intimacy, she began to break down the wall of denial. Her hesitancy as a child to break the "family secret," to maintain her "motherly" responsibilities, and to strive for perfection helped her survive amidst chaos and dysfunction. Yet, she learned that these patterns isolate her in the present, despite her longing for connection. Her understanding of her childhood, shaped in part by her father's alcoholism, her willingness to share her story, and her interdependence with others frame her identity development and recovery process.

Felice's journey and the literature examine some of the experiences and identity development (which is closely linked to recovery) of many traditional-aged adult daughters of alcoholics in college. This research has several implications for student affairs educators who may work with this population of students. Many of the following recommendations are specific to adult daughters, but I feel that the entire population of ACOAs may benefit from these suggestions.

Gaining the gift of self calls for interdependence. Support and encouragement for this task can be enhanced by student affairs educators. Belenky et al (1986) stated that the purpose of education is to assist students in their development. As student affairs educators, it is important to recognize the challenges that adult daughters face in their development.

Additionally, difficulties often become more compounded for adult daughters who feel that they are in a double bind. They are pulled by the family to remain isolated and pulled internally to emphasize connection. By becoming aware of the challenges that adult daughters face in college, educators can be better prepared to challenge and support their development.

Educators must more fully understand the dual conflict daughters face as they search for their sense of self. Educators should encourage these women in an empowering, not paternalistic or maternalistic, way to become involved in group activities (e.g., clubs, organizations, intramurals). These activities can enhance the connection that may provide a safe environment for adult daughters to begin their recovery process and, ultimately, move toward self-definition and self-acceptance.

As Ann and Holly served as role models for Felice, other student affairs educators should recognize the value of role modeling for adult daughters. Many of these women grew up in the environment that provided poor role models. These unhealthy role models are the only individuals after whom adult daughters know to pattern their adult behavior. Because of this, it is vital that educators model healthy behaviors to guide young adults.

Ackerman (1983) and Crawford and Phyfer (1988) identified several roles for educators as they work with adult daughters. First, educators should focus on in service training. Not only should individual educators learn about the issues that surround adult daughters, they should educate others within the profession about this population and strategies that serve to challenge, support, and validate the experiences of these women.

Second, educators should develop resources and serve as referral agents for students. This means that the campus should provide a variety of opportunities for support groups (including single-sex and coeducational groups), individual counseling, and links to community programs. Not all adult daughters need or want to use these resources, but educators should provide the opportunities for those who do. While support resources can be costly, a strong link to community support groups can alleviate the fiscal pressures and still provide a vehicle to discuss and address the experiences of adult daughters.

Third, educators need to provide policy support which implies a commitment to the growth and development of adult daughters on campus. This may include developing grant proposals for outreach, providing money for speakers, and providing reference materials.

Fourth, educators should provide direct service in counseling and programmatic roles. Educators are trained and prepared to listen empathetically and encourage students to work on their issues. Through these skills, those in student affairs can empower individuals to enhance their positive attributes and minimize the negative ones. As programmers, educators can creatively increase campus sensitivity of the issues of adult daughters and discuss methods to confront these concerns.

Educators should continue to conduct research about the population of adult daughters on campus. Because of the limited research about adult daughters, calls for research that generally address adult children of alcoholics should also specifically examine gender differences. Some of the issues that need to be addressed by research include additional empirical data on adult children (Crawford & Phyfer, 1988); the gender differences of the alcoholic parent (Ackerman, 1989; El-Guebaly & Offord, 1977); and the relationships between children and the non-alcoholic parent.

Much of the current literature is deterministic, suggesting that all children fall into certain roles as a result of growing up in an alcoholic family (e.g., Black, 1981; Cermak, 1988; and Kinosian, 1987). Therefore, research should be conducted to identify patterns and themes that adult children may experience, but should not generalize experiences to the entire population of adult children. Furthermore, there is a need for additional research about adult children who are not as adversely affected by the disease of alcoholism (El-Guebaly & Offord, 1977).

The definition of recovery as a gift of self can enhance the work educators do with any student. Receiving one's self is a process that everyone undergoes; although for some, like adult daughters, it may pose greater challenges than for others. This suggests that many of the strategies educators can use may enhance the growth and development of all students, who may or may not be adult daughters. Felice's journey and the review of the literature reflect on the processes of identity development and recovery. It is my intent that this research promotes optimism and hope for all educators who work with students who are "finding themselves" and "recovering."

Conclusions

Felice's journey is still progressing. Healing is a process filled with successes and setbacks. As she moves along, each footstep marks a place on the path. Her footsteps of courage, trust, intimacy, control, and a childhood lost are often intertwined.

Felice's experiences in college helped her discover who she is, especially the strength and power of being a woman. Her self-awareness and changes from old patterns of behavior, like keeping the family secret and distancing herself from others, however slowly they may have emerged, mark healing and recovery from the alcoholic family system.

Although Felice is starting to reconcile the loss of her childhood while her father was at home, she is more recently confronting the loss of another part of her past. Her mother's new marriage marks the closure of a time when she felt she had found part of her childhood. She longs to feel happy for her mother, yet she is in the process of saying goodbye again to a childhood that she feels ended prematurely. This recent loss indicates that Felice's journey is not over, that she will continue on her journey of healing.

Felice still confronts challenges, sometimes taking steps back, sometimes moving forward, often including others in her journey. She finds strength in the unconditional trust of journey. She also finds strength in the unconditional trust of her Higher Power. This spiritual energy helps her to trust herself, to take risks to trust others, and to let go when she faces an obstacle that is not her's to overcome. She has moved from a strong, independent child/woman to a strong, interdependent woman. For Felice, her journey of healing, marked by her footsteps, is a journey worth taking.

References

Ackerman, R. J. (1983). *Children of alcoholics: A guidebook for educators, therapists, and parents* (2nd ed.). Holmes Beach, FL: Learning Publications.

Ackerman, R. J. (1989). *Perfect daughters: Adult daughters of alcoholics.* Deerfield Beach, FL: Health Communications

Belenky, J. F., Clinchy, B. M., Goldberger, N. R., & Tarule, J. M. (1986). *Women's ways of knowing: The development of self, voice, and mind.* New York, NY: Basic Books.

Benson, C. S., & Heller, K. (1987). Factors in the current adjustment of your adult daughters of alcoholic and program drinking fathers. *Journal of Abnormal Psychology, 56,* 305–312.

Berkowitz, A., & Perkins, H. W. (1988). Personality characteristics of children of alcoholics. *Journal of Counseling and Clinical Psychology, 56*(2), 206–209.

Black, C. (1981). *"It will never happen to me!"* New York, NY: Ballantine Books.

Black, C. (1990). *Double duty: Dual dynamics within the chemically dependent home.* New York, NY: Ballantine Books.

Brown, S. (1988). *Treating adult children of alcoholics: A development perspective.* New York, NY: John Wiley & Sons.

Cermak, T. L. (1988, September/October). The road to recovery for adult children of alcoholics. *New Realities,* pp. 24–28, 51–53.

Chickering, A. (1969). *Education and identity* (1st ed.). San Francisco, CA: Jossey-Bass.

Clair, D., & Genest, M. (1987). Variables associated with the adjustment of offspring of alcoholic fathers. *Journal of Studies on Alcohol, 48,* 345–355.

Crawford, R. L., & Phyfer, A .Q. (1988). Adult children of alcoholics: A counseling model. *Journal of College Student Development, 29,* 105–11.

Downing, N. E., & Walker, M. E. (1987). A psychoeducational group for adult children of alcoholics. *Journal of Counseling and Development*, *65*, 440–442.

El-Guebaly, N., & Offord, D. R. (1977). The offspring of alcoholics: A critical review. *American Journal of Counseling and Development*, *134*(40, 357–365.

Ely, M. with Anzul, M., Friedman, T., Garner, D., & Steinmetz, A.M. (1991). *Doing qualitative research: Circles within circles.* New York, NY: Falmer Press.

Filstead, W., McElfresh, O., & Anderson, C. (1981). Comparing the family environments of alcoholic and "normal" families. *Journal of Alcohol and Drug Education*, *26*, 24–31.

Fischer, J. L., Spann, L., & Crawford, D. (1991). Measuring codependency. *Alcoholism Treatment Quarterly*, *8*(1), 87–100.

Friel, J., & Friel, L. (1988). *Adult children: The secrets of dysfunctional families.* Deerfield Beach, FL: Health Communications.

Gilligan, C. (1982). *In a different voice.* Cambridge, MA: Harvard University Press.

Goodman, R. W. (1987). Adult children of alcoholics. *Journal of Counseling and Development*, *66*(4), 162–163.

Gravitz, H. L., & Bowden, J. D. (1985). *Guide to recovery: A book for adult children of alcoholics.* Holmes Beach, FL: Learning Publications.

Guinta, C. (1992). *Fear of intimacy in adult daughters of alcohol abusing and/or psychiatrically distressed mothers and fathers.* Unpublished doctoral dissertation, The University of Vermont, Burlington, VT.

Josselson, R. (1987). *Finding herself: Pathways to identity development in women.* San Francisco, CA: Jossey-Bass.

Kinosian, J. (1987, January). Adult children of alcoholics. *Orange Coast Magazine*, pp. 44–46.

Levenson, R. W., Oyama, O. N., & Meek, P. S. (1987). Greater reinforcement from alcohol for those at risk: Parental risk, personality risk, and gender. *Journal of Abnormal Psychology*, *96*, 242–253.

Lincoln, Y., & Guba, E. (1985). *Naturalistic inquiry.* Newbury Park, CA: Sage Publications.

Lincoln, Y., & Guba, E. (1986). But is it rigorous? Trustworthiness and authenticity in naturalistic inquiry. In D. Williams (Ed.), *Naturalistic evaluation* (pp. 73–84). San Francisco, CA: Jossey-Bass.

Manning, K. (1997). Authenticity in constructivist inquiry: Methodological considerations without prescription. *Qualitative Inquiry*, *3*(1), 93–115.

May, D., & Maniacek, M.A. (1987). Effects of co-dependency on adult children of alcoholics. *Alcoholism*, *23*(1-2), 51–55.

Rearden, J. J., & Markwell, B. S. (1989). Self-concept and drinking problems of college students raised in alcohol abused homes. *Addictive Behaviors*, *14*, 225–227.

Seixas, J. S., & Youcha, G. (1985). *Children of alcoholism: A survivor's manual*. New York, NY: Crown Publishers.

Woititz, J. G. (1983). *Adult children of alcoholics*. Deerfield Beach, FL: Health Communications.

8

You Know I'm Triracial, Right?

Multiracial Student Identity Development and the College Experience

Tim Wilson

America is in the midst of a biracial baby-boom (Root, 1992). Consider the following:

1. For every 100 births to Japanese parents in the United States, there are 139 births to a Japanese and a non-Japanese parent (Ragaza in Matsumoto, 1995).

2. Since 1960, the number of interracial marriages in the United States has risen 547% (Frisby, 1996).

3. It is estimated that 70% to 80% of African Americans possess some level of European ancestry (Zack, 1993).

4. In the majority of Black/White interracial, heterosexual marriages, the woman is White and the man is Black. If and when the couple decides to have children, they will be classified according to the race of the mother (Graham, 1996). In cases where both parents are non-White, the child

is classified according to the race of the father (Chideya, 1995). Such practices have significant impact upon the maintenance of health records (Graham), as well as the monitoring of certain legislation (Fernández, 1996).

5. The last census which included biracial people took place in 1920. Because of social customs such as hypodescent (i.e., assigning racially mixed people to the racial group in their heritage with the least social status) (Root, 1996) and monoracism (i.e., the belief that all people are of one racial background only or at least ought to be) (Wilson, 1997), biracial people have been rendered legally invisible (Zack, 1993). These customs also perpetuate the myths associated with notions of race.

The biracial baby-boomers are growing in numbers and consciousness, and are coming to college. Are our practices, as educators, helping or hindering these students?

Literature Review

Before one can gain insight into the biracial experience, one must consider how U.S. society views race. Americans are obsessed with race, probably because one's race is a key component in determining how a person will be treated by society. Race is a social construct comprised of and driven by law and social custom (López, 1996; Matsumoto, 1995). Race establishes a pecking order in regard to who has access to social, economic, and political power (People's Institute for Survival and Beyond, 1995). In the United States, Whites are at the top of this pecking order and people of color are at the bottom.

America's racial system operates under a divide and conquer mentality (Takaki, 1993). The more isolated the people at the bottom of the hierarchy are, the easier to maintain control and power. In order to do this, boundaries between groups must exist. Each person living under such a system must be categorized into one group and one group only. These classifications, based on physical features (e.g., skin color; shape of one's eyes, nose, lips, etc.), provide the framework for how society will treat him or her. By their very existence, multiracial people confound the system because their physical features may suggest one race, but they may identify with a different race.

The topic of racial self-identification has grown in intensity over the past few years. In an attempt to streamline the information it was receiving during the 1970s, the United States Office of Management and Budget developed Directive 15. This directive requires all public and private sector agencies to design their racial query forms in such a way that the information provided fit into one of five main categories: White, Black, Hispanic, Asian or Pacific Islander, and American Indian or Native Alaskan (Fernández, 1996). Census policy requires that people marking "other" on racial query forms be assigned monoracial categories. If multiple categories are listed, the Census Bureau must list the first classification marked. "Multiracial" or "mixed" responses require a visit by a census taker to obtain a monoracial response. This visit is known as an "eyeball test" because the census taker literally marks the racial classification he or she believes a person to be by looking at him or her (Graham, 1996). In order to avoid such visits, a biracial person must "check one box only", thus denying a part of himself or herself.

There is a growing awareness among biracial people of what it means to be biracial in a society requiring compulsive monoraciality. Groups dedicated to helping biracial men and women articulate and make sense of their experience are forming in communities and on college campuses across the nation (Graham, 1996; Williams, Nakashima, Kich, & Daniel, 1996). A grassroots effort to add a "multiracial" category to the Directive 15 racial classifications is well underway. To date, there are seven states with legislation requiring the inclusion of such an option (Ards, 1997). These are positive steps in that they help broaden our notions of race by acknowledging the fact that racial groups are not naturally occurring, distinct entities. However, the fact remains that most people are ignorant of, ambivalent about, or hostile toward the experience and/or existence of biracial people in America. How does a biracial person develop a positive racial identity in such a society?

Identity Development

Kich (1992) outlined biracial identity development from childhood through adulthood. Three major stages were articulated: initial awareness of differentness and dissonance between self-perceptions and the perceptions of others; struggle for acceptance from others; and self-acceptance as a person with biracial and bicultural identity.

Stage One: Awareness of Differentness and Dissonance

Differentness is a neutral concept, while dissonance implies a negative judgement of difference. The early awareness that one is biracial establishes an awareness of being different. "What are you?," a common question of biracial people, is particularly troubling during this stage.

For many biracial people, their first memories of differentness and dissonance come "during the earliest phases of their transition into peer and reference groups outside of the family, usually between the ages of three and ten. In these experiences, biracial people felt as if they didn't belong to either of their comparison groups" (Kich, 1992, p. 307). Devaluing differentness makes the experience of not belonging more complex. Appearances, names, racially different parents, or birthplaces different from the majority norm increase the ways in which biracial people are marginalized. Internalizing the experiences of discrepancy, ambiguity, and rejection results in self-negation for a biracial person. This occurs because of the negative social and community definitions of the biracial experience, an experience that many people do not understand and, consequently, reject.

Parents play a crucial role in helping a child develop the structure and language necessary to make sense of his or her experiences as he or she develops a healthy self-concept and positive self-esteem. "In valuing each of the child's racial and ethnic heritages, parents structure emotional safety and confidence through a positive interracial label and through modeling an ability to discuss racial and ethnic differences openly" (Kich, 1992, p. 308). Open communication about race and interracial labels validate and foster a child's initial biracial self-concept. Parents can provide this structure through support, open and comfortable communication on feelings, and racial and cultural facts and experiences. A parent's openness about racial and ethnic experiences can provide an understanding of the social devaluation of differentness.

Stage Two: Struggle for Acceptance

This stage often takes place within the context of school or the general community. As children have interactions away from parents and extended family, they become aware of how they and their families are viewed by others. "They want to be known yet are often ashamed and outraged at being so persistently judged in their differentness" (Kich, 1992, p. 310). In this stage, biracial people want to be accepted and hope no one asks about their names or appearances. After answering questions and feeling some level of acceptance by others, a bittersweet sense of triumph is all that remains. People have taken an interest in the biracial person, but the same "What are you?" questions are asked. Once again, parents can play a major role in alleviating a biracial person's level of isolation and embarrassment about him or herself and the family's racial difference.

The tension between being loyal to one's parents and the desire to be accepted by school friends often intensifies the need to separate home and school life. While the family can be seen as a refuge from the possibility of peer group rejection, it is also the source of differentness. Because dissonant experiences are hard to resolve during this time, biracial people tend to compartmentalize themselves as a way to resolve conflicting loyalty and gain acceptance. Because biracial people embody dual racial origins, they are constantly reminded of their interracial situation and compartmentalization is only a temporary defense against fears of rejection.

In Kich's (1992) study, one of the more difficult struggles biracial people had to resolve was identifying with one parent or the other, a situation often appearing as a question of competing loyalties. In this stage, an ambivalent relationship was formed with the parent most personifying the person's experience of differentness and an over-identification with the other parent. Feelings of embarrassment, disappointment, or self-doubt were suppressed, while frustration, anger, longing, and fear of inferiority played themselves out in choosing one parent or the other.

The struggle for acceptance is intensified by typical adolescent conflicts, resulting in an attempt to isolate home from social life. By the end of high school, the biracial person not only learns about and uses a specific label for him or herself, but is more aware of his or her parents' heritages as valuable aspects of themselves and their roots. By being involved with the extended family, a self-awareness stretching across generations helps increase a biracial person's confidence in such an identity. As time goes on, biracial people make a more active and conscious effort to choose sides, thus intensifying their experience. This choice, no longer exploratory, is often based on their convictions and emerging assertion of a biracial identity. In this stage biracial people make a clear distinction between themselves and their parents, and are aware of their parents' unresolved issues. By recognizing and accepting themselves as interracial people, they are also starting to see themselves as more firmly belonging to a different racial category than either parent.

Stage Three: Self Acceptance and Assertion of
an Interracial Identity

The biracial person's ability to create self-definitions as opposed to being defined by the perceptions, definitions and stereotypes of others is the major achievement of biracial identity development. "This ability to define him-or-herself positively is an important reversal of the social construction of a previous identity as devalued, unacceptable, and anomalous" (Kich, 1992, p. 314).

In this stage, acceptance of a biracial identity usually occurs after high school and is more concrete during and after college or occupational transitions. Biracial people begin to understand that not all inquiries and inquirers are racists, intent on defining them negatively. Where they once felt the need to please or provoke, biracial people are now able to measure their answers to their needs as well as the needs of the situation. Biracial people also begin to actively seek out biracial others, as well as those in other racial and ethnic groups. They want uninhibited contact, free from "full explanation" of their heritage. During this stage, biracial people come to value their identity as something "constructed out of the relationship between personal experience and social meanings of ethnicity, race and group membership. The simple assertion of being who they are, of being biracial, is the developmental achievement of this ongoing and unfinished process" (Kich, 1992, p. 316).

This knowledge base obtained from the literature provides a theoretical context in which to place the research conducted with a multiracial undergraduate student. The methodology used for this study and the resulting case study are contained in the next sections.

Methodology

I had known my respondent, "Res" [a pseudonym], for over a year before embarking on this project. I asked him to participate because I found him to be bright, confident, and articulate. We met for five interviews over the course of a semester. In our first meeting, we co-constructed a consent form which outlined the purposes of the project and articulated the possible uses of the data collected. During this meeting I guaranteed his anonymity (even though he was not concerned about my using his name).

Data Collection and Analysis

Notes consisting of key words and phrases were taken during our conversations which were converted into field notes. The respondent member checked (Manning, 1997) each set of notes, as well as my analytical memos (Glaser & Strauss, 1967) which contained interpretations of the meaning expressed during the interviews. Throughout the process, Res consistently commented that the notes and interpretations were accurate. Any discrepancies between what he meant and what I wrote or interpreted were quickly remedied. By the third interview, consistent patterns and themes emerged within the data. I knew I could end the data collection stage of the research when the data repeated (Lincoln & Guba, 1985).

Case Study Voice

A qualitative researcher is charged with the task of telling someone's story in that person's voice. This case study is written in the first-person in order to achieve that objective. Like many qualitative researchers, I want you to live vicariously through Res' words. Almost every word in this case study was spoken by him during the interviews. Some words and phrases were added to clarify his statements. I hope that you will experience a range of emotions while reading this and that these words will move you to a new level of understanding.

Qualitative research has been called "me-search" (Ely, Anzul, Friedman, Garner, & Steinmetz, 1991). That is, qualitative researchers explore topics that are somehow reflective of themselves. I am no different. Because of this, member checking, peer debriefing, and audits, both internal and external, (Manning, 1997) were most helpful in the development of the final version of this case.

Focus of the Study

The focus of this study was to determine how a biracial person develops his or her racial identity in a monoracial setting. I wanted to discover the factors influencing the identity development process of biracial students. I was curious about whether it is possible to possess a biracial identity which acknowledges the race of both parents. Additionally, I wanted to know the ways in which the college experience helps and hinders the racial identity process for biracial students.

My interest in this topic goes beyond the scope of this study. I have written research papers, including a masters thesis on this topic, and read extensively on multiracial identity. I mention this because, at times, I enhance the information I gained from my respondent with information from this knowledge base.

I enjoyed conducting this case study for two reasons. First and foremost, my respondent and I got along well and he definitely made my job as a researcher easy because he could articulate his experiences without much prompting. The topic of this study also helped expand my insights as to the literature I had explored. While this was helpful, I had to make sure that my interview questions were grounded in the focus of my study and in where my respondent was leading me, not in the a priori library research. If my respondent's answers were different from the literature, the potential existed for me to discount his voice in favor of the "experts." I had to remember that this study was about him, not the existing literature on multiracial identity.

Authenticity and Trustworthiness

A high quality study was achieved through a co-constructed consent form, member checking activities of all of interview notes and the case study. The respondent expressed several times his enjoyment of talking about being triracial and that he would like to hear my insights on the subject after the study. Over the course of five interviews, persistent observation was achieved.

Verstehen or deep understanding of how he achieved his multiracial identity and how his college experience impacts that identity was achieved through our multiple interviews and the intensity of those conversations. I maintained an accurate audit trail so that data can be traced back to its source. Peer debriefing activities were conducted throughout the course of the research process. These peers reviewed the interview notes, gave advice on possible themes, and gave feedback on the interpretations.

When two people enter into an interracial marriage, those opposed to the idea often ask "but what about the children?" (Funderburg, 1994) This case study presents the thoughts and feelings of a young man who is the offspring of such a union. Growing up in a Black household, my parents would sometimes tease my siblings and I when we caught them in a no-win argument by saying, "Hush now, grown folks is talkin'. Children are meant to be seen, not heard." In this case study, the child will answer the question, "what about the children?" While the grown folk might be seen, in this case study they will definitely not be heard. Draw close and pay attention. The child is about to speak.

The Case Study

Res is a second-year undergraduate student studying political science. He attends a mid-sized, public university in the Northeast and is active in co-curricular organizations. Most of the interviews for this case study were conducted in his residence hall room. On the walls, I noticed Res and his roommate had two posters of Bob Marley, an Ansel Adams poster ("The Mural Project, 1941–1942"), and a "seeing eye" poster with a yellow star in the middle. A small fish tank sat atop a cluttered desk. Two small goldfish raced around the artificial environment of their humming, cylindrical home. On the left, I noticed pictures on the wall. Many of them centered around themes of achievement, particularly graduation, as well as a picture of Res on a water ride at Six Flags. I saw a picture of Res' mother, the "Watermill Boys" and his siblings. . . . "These pictures look so professional." "Yeah, we model." I also noticed two well-used football helmets, one sitting on a desk and another on a shelf above the two-seater couch. "I didn't really like football that much but I was big and I could do it, so I played. My favorite sport . . . is volleyball."

You Know I'm Triracial, Right?

I was born in Rockville Centre, on Long Island and raised in Queens. I remember very little about my childhood. I remember where I lived and my best friend. . . . He was Latino. We lived there until I was six. Then we moved to California. My mother is from Vietnam and her sister came to California from Vietnam. So my father, being the good person he is, moved the family out to California so my mom could be near her sister. We lived in San Francisco for a while. . . . We lived mostly in Sacramento though, until I was about 13. It was the first time I was able to see my relatives, who were people of color, and I loved it. I didn't see any differences, beyond the superficial, between whites and nonwhites. In 1989, we moved to Southampton, Long Island. We live on the Shinnecock Indian Reservation. . . . My father is Native American and African American. We've been there for about seven years. I never asked why we moved and my parents never talked about it. My opinion of the whole thing is that we had been away for a long time and I didn't know that much about my Native heritage. Economically, it was a good time to move back.

My parents never had to sit me down and say, "you're this, this, this and this." Since I was able to comprehend race, I just knew who I was. I always knew I was different from the other kids in my school because of my hair, my skin color. In our house in California and at my house in New York, we had two portraits of Natives in full regalia . . . above the fireplace. . . . I'd ask questions about the pictures on the walls and that would lead into stories about them and my family. We had Vietnamese poetry on the walls and African statues from when my aunt went to Africa. We had lots of ethnic stuff reflecting the cultures I am. My parents took me to a couple of Kwanzaa celebrations when we lived in California. Events like that keyed me into my background.

You know I'm triracial, right? Some people ask "what are you?" This comes from ignorance. I don't mean this in a negative way, but it's true. Whites tend to say, "what are you?" and that's so dehumanizing. The term "what" is what's dehumanizing about it. "What" usually refers to things, inanimate objects. No one asks "who" I am or "how do you identify yourself?" When people ask this way, it makes me feel human, more comfortable. When people ask this way, it makes me think they have thought before they have spoken. As far as the external world is concerned, I'm an "it" as opposed to a person. I'm looked at by non-ALANA [African American, Latino, Native American, Asian American] people as one of a greater cohort rather than as an individual with three racial backgrounds. It's very superficial, unless they're self-righteous. People of color will ask more questions. I hear stuff like, "Well, you don't seem like you're all Mexican" and they'll ask me about my background to try and find out who I am.

You know I'm triracial, right? When I applied to schools, I checked "Native American." I avoided "Asian American" because many college administrators feel Asians are a threat. . . . If I check "Asian," they have a picture of what I look like and how I can achieve. I avoid "African American" because they are the most visibly oppressed group in the nation. I checked "Native

American" because of the passive stereotype. Natives are the most invisibly oppressed group. Also, Natives get more financial aid than anyone else.

If a person is triracial, biracial, multiracial, whatever, I don't think they should have to choose one [race] to make society feel better. If race really didn't matter, the category wouldn't exist. It's not a good feeling to live in a society where race matters. I have to make a choice as to what group I acknowledge. When I do that, I have to ignore the work and sacrifices others have made to get me where I am right now. Not acknowledging other parts of my ethnicity erases a part, well, two whole parts of my family and cultures that mean a lot to me. It doesn't make me feel like shit, like I can't do anything in my life. I'm not selling out. I'm playing the system to survive and make something of myself. I still recognize the other ethnicities and I don't weigh one more than the other, but I'm doin' what I gotta do.

Would I support a "multiracial" category on census and school forms? Well, like I said . . . I don't think the [race] category should exist. If the category serves no purpose, what is it for? If states or the government feel the need to have it, then yes, I support a multiracial classification. Then people wouldn't have to choose. Being forced to choose one race demeans the past struggles of the others. The multiracial category is a good thing because then I won't have to choose anymore. I'd use it unless I found a reason not to.

You know I'm triracial, right? Being triracial makes me a better rounded person because I recognize and celebrate every culture running within my veins. It means I come from a well-rounded, more diverse background than most. It means I'm more fortunate than most because I can compare the cultures of my family and can witness and participate in them. Being triracial is really cool. People can be really boring, just White or European or Caucasian or whatever . . . but to be triracial. I have so much history to look back on. It's cool to celebrate so many cultures and realize they're all you. It used to be that if someone questioned my ethnicity, I used to get defensive. Now people can say what they want. I know who I am. Any man who's questioned is going to get defensive. That's part of being a man. Being triracial has made me more, and I hate this word, sensitive and perceptive about things going on around me in terms of race and stuff like that.

Does skin color matter to me when it comes to dating? No. Some people, and I find this more with women of color . . . would rather me not date White women because I'm a person of color. Some feel I am blinded by sex and they don't consider why I might be dating a White woman. They might think we're dating because she thinks I'm exotic and different or something. My ex-girlfriend Jessica was White. She and I used to have the best conversations about everything, especially race relations. We had a lot of sex and connected on the intellectual level, too. That was the great thing about our relationship. One day, I said, "I love you." She asked why and I broke it down for her. She said, "Well, I don't think I feel the same way, but I'm falling in love with you." We eventually broke up. I'm in a relationship with a woman right now. We have sex and everything, but we don't have the same intellectual connection.

I had some really good, supportive friends last year and they were really helpful when Jessica and I broke up. I didn't have a lot of friends in high school. I had lots of acquaintances and people would tell me I was popular, but I didn't have a lot of "friends." That hasn't really changed since I came to college. I define a "friend" as one I can confide in. A person I can talk to, someone that will judge me by the content of my character . . . with acceptance comes friendship. This is my opinion: if I accept someone, they can potentially be my friend. When I'm with my friends . . . I can vent and know that it will stay with them. I find acceptance with my friends, like my good friend Tracey. My fraternity is another place [where I could find acceptance], but it's not there yet.

I'm accepted on different levels with different people. With . . . non-ALANA people, they tend to say, "Oh, we have a 'minority' here." I have a 'special privilege pass' like OJ or like Colin Powell. With ALANA people . . . they tend to think, "well, there's one more person of color, and the more the better." They also tend to see me as a good leader. You want to know about the "special privilege pass?" Well, and I find this more with Whites, people tend to say "you're not like the others." I defy stereotypes. For example, if I'm with a group of people and someone says something derogatory toward African Americans . . . like "Oh, those people are lazy." I'll say "Well, I'm part African American." Then that person'll say, "Well, you're not like them. You're involved. You get good grades." I'm like a fly on the wall, just taking it all in.

Back home, my friends and I have what this state would call a "gang." We call ourselves "The Watermill Boys." There are four of us: one Jewish guy, two Caucasians, and one person of color,

*me. I hang out with a friend of mine that lives in Watermill. It's
the next town over from mine. One day, we were hangin' out at
my friend's house, playin' pool and we said "we're the Watermill
Boys" and that's how we got our name. We were looking for ways
to . . . what's that word that starts with a "C?" It means to solidify your relationship. . . ."Consummate." That's it. We were
looking for ways to consummate our relationship. We thought
about something like permanent tattoos. We all really liked smoking cigars. . . . Anyway, Mark and Mo went down to Schwarzeneg-
ger's cigar store in New York and bought these lighters. . . . Mark
and Mo bought these lighters and they're identical. There were
only four lighters like this in the store. We got them engraved,
"WMB 8-96." It's got two flames on it because, you know, cigars
tend to be thick.*

*I couldn't afford the lighter and I told them to just go ahead
and do it without me because I can't afford it. But they bought it
for me anyway. I'm gonna pay them back. They don't know it yet,
but I'm gonna pay them back. This lighter cost $210. It's gold.
For them to spend $840 on lighters and pay for mine when I
couldn't afford it, I figure that's got to be something. It's got to
be friendship. After we got the lighters, we went down to the
beach, smoked some cigars, and drank some brews because we
were all going to college.*

*My friend John goes to Dartmouth. Since my freshman year in
high school, I knew I wanted to go to Dartmouth. I'm Dartmouth
material. I wanted to go because it was an Ivy League school
and I had relatives that went there . . . also because of its Native
background. I heard about it from relatives and friends. I used to
flip through the college catalogs when I was a freshman in high
school and it just appealed to me. During my senior year, I applied for early decision. The admissions director at Dartmouth
came to my school and talked to my guidance counselor. My guidance counselor told me, "You're basically in. All you have to do
is fill out your application and you're in." So me, being my cocky
self told everybody, well not everybody but a few people, that I
was in at Dartmouth. I filled out the application and sent it in
and got an interview.*

*My interview went well. I knew everyone on the committee. Well,
April rolls around and Res gets rejected . . . . I was really hurt.
I don't know if you know how it works there, but there is a committee of five people who decide and they have to be unanimous
when they vote. When it came to me, there were four thumbs up
and one down, which makes me feel a little better. My grades*

weren't the best. I had a lot of activities, but my grades weren't as good as some of the other people applying to Dartmouth. I still want to go to Dartmouth. I might apply as a transfer. Statistically, I'll have a better chance as a transfer. I also applied to USC [University of Southern California] because it has a great law program and volleyball team, but I didn't get in there either, so I came here.

You know I'm triracial right? This school has helped me in ways they don't even know. They've helped by not knowing they were helping me. Doing the negative stuff they do [to people of color] has helped me develop who I am in terms of my racial backgrounds. By the color of my skin, I'm going to be discriminated against, so right there, I don't think I'm any different than a dark skinned person of color. I mean, society can deal with me in one of two ways. They can say, "Oh, he's a person of color, so fuck 'im." Or they can say "Wow! He's triracial. He's so exotic. That's neat!!" This mostly comes from White people. People of color are like, "Okay, that's cool."

As a student, being triracial has been positive and negative. Like last year, we had death threats and stuff and I had to let my schoolwork go so I could be there for other people of color. Since people have a lot of stereotypes and think I'm lazy or no good, that pushes me to do better as a student. In terms of developing as a multiracial man, being in an all White state has forced me to acknowledge my racial background. Last year, I was influenced a lot by people of color on campus. They raised my awareness and consciousness about racial issues. I've learned a lot about institutional racism. I realize the injustices done against me and other people of color.

Remember when I was talking about Dartmouth and how I still wanted to go? Well, people say I should go for myself, but I'm not so sure. If Martin Luther King, Jr. and Malcolm X did what was good for them, they never would have been assassinated. This school's problems make me want to stay. After the seniors leave this year . . . who will be around? I'm active because it establishes connections. Connections are the key to the world. Power comes with connections . . . I'm a very political person. If I leave, things may take a negative turn here for people. I'm not saying I'm the best leader but I've seen a lot and dealt with a lot of things here. If sacrificing Dartmouth is what I have to do to promote equality here, than that's what I'll do.

What kind of support do I receive from Multicultural Student Affairs? Last year, I had more support from the office because the staff was all people of color and they knew how I felt. This year, the staff is greatly reduced and is not all people of color. If I needed a tutor or something like that, I could go into the office and find one. They've been very supportive like that. But last year, I could go in for social or academic problems. This year, a lot of the more active students who were able to help me out are gone. This year, a few people are still around but I find that I have to reach into myself a lot for empowerment. I hang out a lot with students of color. You know how it is when we hang out. That helps empower me too.

This is bad, but I don't concentrate on myself. I like doing for other people. I've always been sympathetic to people's feelings, situations. I want to make people happy. I realize I'm a privileged person. There are people who aren't nowhere near where I am in life and I'm not very high. It's easier to make someone cry than it is to make them laugh. People say I'm a clown, but I like to make them feel good . . . boost their self esteem. There's a lot of people who feel like shit and they shouldn't have to.

What would I do if I could change things here for multiracial students? That's hard because not all multiracial students may feel the same way as me. I might say they should start more support groups for multiracial students, but other multiracial students might say "I'm fine, leave me alone." I think one thing that could be done would be to get more students of color here, period. Having an increased voice as to what goes on here and to be recognized as such would also help. We aren't recognized and we don't have much of a voice, so the university can basically do whatever it wants.

Findings

Being Exoticized

On two occasions, Res spoke of being "exoticized" by other students. He discussed how some women of color assume he is dating a White woman because he may be blinded by sex. And the White woman may see his triracial-ness as being exotic, something out of the ordinary. Because his multiracial identity is "unusual" (even though many peoples of the world have a long history of interracial mixture), this may add an edge of excitement. The second occasion was in reference to how he believes he is perceived by some people at his college. Uniqueness, as opposed to a sexual exoticization, seems to be the context in this second account.

Identity Development and Its Articulation

On more than one occasion, Res articulated his pride in being multiracial and showed that it *is* possible to acknowledge and celebrate more than one racial identity. He has an exceptional ability to reflect upon and articulate his experience as a multiracial man. Res is an individual with a well-developed, multiracial identity. This identity has helped him survive, not only as a multiracial man, but as a person of color. This identity was created in part with the help of his parents who openly shared the aspects of his multidimensional ethnicity. Since childhood, Res knew he was different from other children. His parents' willingness to openly discuss the aspects of his triracial-ness helped him develop an understanding of who he was and what it was that made him unique. This sharing also helped him become comfortable with his triracial identity and helped him develop a vocabulary for his experience. His ability to put language to the meaning of his identity and experience is key to his ability to articulate his experience.

Res is a person who plays the hand he is dealt. Our system of racial classification forces people to choose only one racial category when asked to self-identify. Such a system forces multiracial people to choose one aspect of their racial identity over another. While Res is far from happy about having to choose only one aspect of his racial background for official purposes, he has chosen to focus his dissatisfaction by using the system to his advantage. Race is something that is done to people (King & DaCosta, 1996). By this I mean that racial identifications have absolute, stereotypical behavioral descriptions attached to them (e.g., all Asian Americans are good in math). These descriptions are consciously and unconsciously used to prejudge people, making life easier or more difficult. As a person of color, race is done to Res.

Because he has such a well-developed sense of his racial selves, Res is a person who "does race" by manipulating the stereotypical notions of his racial backgrounds. He takes advantage of his fluid racial identity by picking out aspects that will help "work the system" to his advantage. Some people might call this selling out. Res says he's doing what he has to in order to survive. If given the opportunity, Res would utilize a multiracial classification category, even though he disagrees with the whole notion of having racial categories on applications. "If race didn't matter, the category wouldn't exist." Having a multiracial category would put an end to his having to sacrifice pieces of who he is in order to "make society feel better." This demonstrates the desire on his part to combine an external wholeness with the internal wholeness he already feels.

Res has two racial personas: one is public and the other is private. Publicly, Res is seen as a person of color and is subsequently treated that way by Whites and by other people of color (unless people ask how he identifies himself). People are able to assume this because of his skin color. He stated that he is often mistaken for being Mexican. Privately, he knows he is triracial. That is, he is a man of African, Native American and Vietnamese descent. The public persona was articulated in our interviews, unless I specifically asked for his insights as a multiracial person. This circumstance could be due to the fact that he has never been empowered to assert a multiracial identity in a monoracial society. His self-knowledge has empowered him to integrate his internal and external selves into a more complete identity. This is more of a private identity because Res, and others like him, do not have the opportunity to officially identify as multiracial.

Friendship and Acceptance

For Res, friendship and acceptance go hand in hand. Both are very important to him as they are safe, non-judgmental, and confidential places. This is especially important, as the racial climate on his campus is often hostile toward students of color. Res is willing to make significant sacrifices for friends and his community. When he spoke of his dream of attending Dartmouth, he also stated his willingness to sacrifice that dream because of racial tensions at his current school. "This is bad but I don't concentrate on myself. I like doing for other people."

This sacrifice theme also presented itself in a story about how some of his close friends decided to obtain symbols of their friendship: identical cigar lighters. The lighters his friends wanted were too expensive for him, but his friends made a sacrifice by purchasing a lighter and having it engraved for him. It seems as though ultimate friendship, for Res, manifests itself in the willingness to make sacrifices for people one cares about.

Triraciality and Other Aspects of Identity

Researchers often limit their work on identity to very specific elements. In this study, I wanted to use racial identity as a means of exploring other aspects of human identity such as gender, sexual orientation, etc. As a man, Res noted that his triracial identity has made him more sensitive about activities going on around him in terms of race. At one point in time, Res noted that he would get defensive if anyone questioned his racial identity. "Any man who's questioned is going to get defensive. That's part of being a man." This indicates that Res once thought that, if questioned, a man had to use what he had in order to prove he was right, to show he was strong. Now, he does not get defensive when asked because he is confident in his identity and knows who he is. Being a triracial man in a predominantly White state has made him more conscious about racial issues and how they impact him and other people of color.

For many people, the choice of a dating partner is as much a means of demonstrating group membership as it is a means of companionship (Twine, 1996). For example, in order to demonstrate that a person is a member of the African American community she or he may consciously seek out African American dating partners. Res does not use such a strategy. He dates people he is attracted to, regardless of race. Some people may not approve, but he does not seem to care.

The College Experience

I assumed that the practices and culture of my respondent's college would have an adverse impact on his identity development. In reacting to his school's homogeneity and hostility to students of color, Res publicly asserted an identity as a student of color before asserting a multiracial identity. This demonstrates the fluid nature of his multiracial identity. The context of each situation determines how he will present himself. If asked how he identifies himself, he will reply that he is of African American, Native American and Vietnamese descent. People seem to translate this multiracial identity into a monoracial classification as a person of color.

Being a triracial student has been both a positive and a negative experience for Res. This setting has only sharpened his sense of self and of how the institution's practices impact him and other students of color. He has stated that the way his university interacts with students of color has made him aware of institutionalized racism. His awareness of these issues came from students and professional staff members at his university.

Res noted that there was a difference in the type of support he felt was coming from his school's Multicultural Student Affairs Office. In his first year, he felt comfortable seeking help from the staff with social and academic problems. This comfort level stemmed from the fact that the office was close to being fully staffed and was comprised of people of color who had an understanding of how he felt as a person of color. This year, he only feels comfortable seeking help for academic issues because the staff is not completely of color and is not at full complement.

One of the most common encounters a multiracial student can experience is the "what are you?" question. Res notes that the way in which this question is asked can make quite a bit of difference. Asking "what are you" is dehumanizing and ignorant in his opinion because the term "what" refers to inanimate objects. He finds that it is much easier to answer such a question if a person phrases it as "how do you identify yourself?" He notes that people of color are more prone to ask how he identifies himself and that whites tend to ask "what" he identifies himself as.

Conclusion

This case study has two implications for higher education. First, Res' frustration with having to segment his racial identity for the sake of a classification scheme and his willingness to utilize a multiracial classification should be further explored. There is a growing consensus among multiracial people for such a classification. Forcing students to choose perpetuates the biological notion of race being naturally occurring and distinct groupings of human beings. In actuality, such groupings are social in nature. These social groupings render multiracial people like Res as "other" or invisible. If universities truly cherish diversity, they will alter the manner in which they do business in order to allow multiracial students to officially acknowledge all aspects of their racial identity *if they choose to do so.* Some multiracial students are content with a monoracial identity. While there is a growing desire for a multiracial classification, the full impact of such a move probably will not be immediately felt because multiracial people have never been given the option to officially identify as anything other than a monoracial person. A multiracial classification merely provides multiracial people with the option of identifying as such. It is in no way mandatory. While such a move may be logistically challenging, it will yield more accurate information as to the racial makeup of a school's student body.

The second implication lies in the way in which people are educated about racial difference. Res' comments and insights about "what are you?" demonstrate the need for student affairs educators to integrate issues of multiracial identity into the content of diversity education. Such a move will challenge the notion of race being an absolute, as opposed to a fluid, aspect of identity and will serve as one more weapon in the fight against racism. Challenging the notion of race as a naturally occurring hierarchy will lead students to critically examine what race really is and what it is really used for. Because professionals working in the area of multicultural affairs are often charged with addressing the needs of students of color as well as educating the campus community, these professionals will have to become more familiar with the issues faced by multiracial students.

References

Ards, A. (1997, February 11). The multiracial movement raises questions about political Black identity. *The Village Voice*, pp. 36, 44.

Chideya, F. (1995). *Don't believe the hype: Fighting cultural misinformation about African-Americans.* New York: Plume.

Fernández, C. (1996). Government classification of multiracial/multiethnic people. In M. Root (Ed.), *The multiracial experience: Racial borders as the new frontier*, (pp. 15–36). Thousand Oaks, CA: Sage.

Frisby, M. K. (1996, January). Black, white, or other. *Emerge, (7),* pp. 48–54.

Funderburg, L. (1994). *Black, white, other.* New York: Quill.

Graham, S. (1996). The real world. In M. Root (Ed.), *The multiracial experience: Racial borders as the new frontier*, (pp. 37–48). Thousand Oaks, CA: Sage.

Kich, G. K. (1992). The developmental process of asserting a biracial, bicultural identity. In M. Root (Ed.), *Racially mixed people in America*, (pp. 304–320). Newbury Park, CA: Sage.

King, R. C. & DaCosta, K. M. (1996). Changing face, changing race: The remaking of race in the Japanese American and African American communities. In M. Root (Ed.), *The multiracial experience: Racial borders as the new frontier*, (pp. 227–244). Thousand Oaks, CA: Sage.

López, I. F. H. (1996). *White by law: The legal construction of race.* New York: New York University Press.

Matsumoto, A. (1995). *Both yet neither: Issues facing Japanese American/European American biracial and bi-ethnic college students.* Unpublished manuscript, The University of Vermont.

People's Institute for Survival and Beyond (1995). Unpublished manuscript. New Orleans, LA: Publisher.

Root, M. (1992). Within, between, and beyond race. In M. Root (Ed.), *Racially mixed people in America*, (pp. 3–11). Newbury Park, CA: Sage.

Takaki, R. (1993). *A different mirror: A history of multicultural America.* Boston, MA: Back Bay Books.

Twine, F. (1996). Heterosexual alliances: The romantic management of racial identity. In M. Root (Ed.), *The multiracial experience: Racial borders as the new frontier*, (pp. 291–304). Thousand Oaks, CA: Sage.

Williams, T. K., Nakashima, C. L., Kich, G. K., and Daniel, G. R. (1996). Being different together in the university classroom: Multiracial identity as transgressive education. In M. Root (Ed.), *The multiracial experience: Racial borders as the new frontier*, (pp. 359–379). Thousand Oaks, CA: Sage.

Wilson, T. (1997). *The multiracial majority: biracial student identity development and the college experience.* Unpublished manuscript, The University of Vermont.

Zack, N. (1993). *Race and mixed race.* Philadelphia: Temple University Press.

9

The Ethics of Evocation

Kathleen Manning

Any research which utilizes others' words and makes claims about truths (even context-dependent ones) can have dangerous consequences. Qualitative researchers take the words of others as data, perform analysis, and publicly present the data as a research product. This product, often a case study, is, by its very definition, different from the original expression by the respondents. Caution therefore must be exercised when qualitative researchers take a person's story and turn his or her words into a public account. The ethical obligation of staying true to the respondents' words, accurately representing their perspective, and faithfully portraying their meaning is profound. Researchers always face the danger of taking someone's personal meaning and turning it to professional use: resident assistant training, professional staff advancement, theory development.

A significant reality of qualitative research is that a researcher can never climb into the shoes of another to fully comprehend the meaning expressed by the respondents. Their words, filtered through the perspective of the researcher, will always be altered—if only ever so slightly. "Interpretation is idiographic in the sense that it is an individual's (the inquirer's) interpretation of individual's (the respondents') interpretation" (Manning, 1989, p. 93). The interpretation expressed in the final case study is always the researcher's interpretation of the respondents' interpretation.

As such, the word, "evocation," is used here to express the idea that the words and accounts in this book are more than a simple restatement or transcription of the data collected. Constructivist inquiry is an interpretive and collaborative methodology. The ethical obligation to the respondent and responsibility of "getting it right" are reflected in the words of Liz Skeffington (personal communication, May 22, 1997), one of the chapter authors.

> As my relationship with the respondent grew, so did the responsibility I felt to co-construct a case study which accurately portrayed the unique experience of the individual . . . To have my respondent tell me that the case study wove together all his scattered thoughts in a clear, meaningful, and gripping way meant more than I can express.

Liz took her experiences with qualitative research and translated the skills learned into administrative practice. The lessons learned were about hearing and attending to the voices that compose student culture.

> Qualitative research taught me how to listen to an individual's voice. [During my study] I was clearly hearing my respondent's, but I was no longer hearing the voices of students who would tell me that drinking was just what college students did. I soon realized that ignoring students' ideas and opinions resulted in an ineffective method for educating students about alcohol use. I was thrown back into reality when I began a literature review which indicated that the vast majority of college students will drink while in college. This motivated me to listen to the voices of all the students around me and ask, "How do you effectively educate students about alcohol?" I have used my experience with qualitative research to answer this ever-illusive question.

For Liz, the positive researcher-respondent relationship became an ideal for administrator-student interaction in her practice.

Implications for Practice and Policy

Several themes, highlighted in Chapter 1, were folded into and discussed in the case studies. These themes include identity; complexity of campus life; links to considerations beyond oneself; complexity, distinctiveness, and dynamism; and expression of unheard, unacknowledged voices. Several of these themes are revisited in this final chapter to bring these ideas full circle in light of the data and interpretations presented in the chapters.

Identity

Identity is an enduring late adolescent challenge and a major feature of campus life. Several of the case studies link the original research presented in the case studies with existing student development theory. The result is an expansion of the boundaries of that theory in significant ways.

Existential Identity

Current student development theory rarely speaks of the existential struggles a traditional college age student encounters with the death of a peer. While many student affairs educators have worked with students during these tragic circumstances, the professional literature provides minimal guidance about the students' challenges during a crisis such as a suicide. The complexity of college life and the crises that are possible are clearly articulated in Ahuna's case study about suicide. Students are no longer, if they ever were, carefree. They struggle with issues of life and death. Existential questions included, "why did he die and I live?" "What is the meaning of life?" and "How do I mourn the death of a friend?" Ahuna's recommendations and the vicarious experience available through reading her case study can assist student affairs educators to more adroitly respond to students' needs during a suicide crisis.

In a similar fashion to Ahuna's case, Skeffington's chapter vividly portraying the struggles of a resident assistant as he works through the alcohol-related death of a resident has similar existential themes. How is a student's identity permanently influenced by experiencing the death of a peer? What does his existence as a survivor mean in relation to the pain that he experiences in working through such a traumatic event? These experiences in the face of crises are permanently etched into a student's identity. These considerations can be part and parcel of identity development theory.

Gender Identity

Student affairs educators are well-versed in gender identity development theory as articulated by Carol Gilligan (1982); Belenky, Clinchy, Golberger, and Tarule (1986); and Baxter Magolda (1992). The nuances of voice informed by culturally-constructed gender experiences is a well-known theme of identity development.

But Regan takes the gender identity themes of voice, connectedness, and relationship a step further by positioning them alongside the power dynamics of sex and rape. Her case is particularly striking because of the student affairs profession's reliance on peer staff to undertake educational efforts concerning rape, AIDS, and sexual harassment. Her case begs consideration of the fact that these students may be struggling with a limited knowledge and experiential base to perform such a task. They may lack the developmental perspective and maturity to carry the burden of educating their peers about these difficult topics.

Professional Identity

The majority of student affairs educators possess the degrees, training, and experience that mark them as professionals. With the casual assumption that educational accomplishments often bring, we can be blinded to the fact that professional expertise is obtained through various means. All professionals can take a lesson from Dee, the university custodian who invited Wong into her nightly domain. She conducts her duties with a level of integrity and personal ethics matched by few, regardless of degrees or power. She teaches students and staff alike significant lessons about dignity in the face of demeaning work conditions and stereotypes. Dee illustrates the wisdom present at all levels of university life—if only we look. She provides answers to the questions about how to form an inclusive, participatory community where arbitrary hierarchical positions could potentially have less meaning.

Identity as Related to Family

Hart's case depicts the ways that a woman, despite the tragedy of alcoholism in her immediate family, can gain independence and the "gift of self." Identity development theory assumes the need for a nurturing environment within which the child can learn to trust and love. An integrated sense of self is dependent on a family environment where consistency rather than arbitrariness creates a climate ripe for growth. Alcoholism shatters any hopes for a trusting, consistent environment. Not knowing whether he or she will come home to a drunk or sober parent, the child becomes overly-dependent on strategies of control and order.

Hart adds nuance to the identity themes of autonomy, relationships, and inter-relatedness by allowing the reader to understand an ACOA's unique struggles. Felice is a triumph of identity development as she works through the denial that accompanies the disease of alcoholism to form an intact self, perhaps because of the strength gained from her experiences within her family of origin.

Multiracial Identity

Wilson argues in Chapter 8 that society dictates monoraciality. This demand to identify oneself according to one racial identity (e.g., African American or White or Asian American) is most clearly expressed by the requirement that students "check only one box" on admissions applications and other institutional documents.

Student affairs development theorists have not articulated the nuances of racial identity development. Borrowing from the counseling field, student affairs educators can fall back on William Cross (1991), Sue and Sue (1990), Lee and Richardson (1991), and Pederson (1988) to assist them with knowledge about the identity development of students of color. Experiences with racism, nuances of cultural expression, and a different experience base result in developmental patterns which, while in some ways resembling the White male students upon which much of the theory was developed, are unique in significant ways (McEwen, Roper, Bryant, & Langa, 1990).

Wilson's respondent, Res, articulately expresses issues of identity development that transcend the "color-blind" and generalized accounts of early student development theory. His case clearly indicates that student affairs educators cannot generalize from a sample of predominantly White college students to all students. Race, gender, class, and the idiosyncrasies of a student's background preclude any easy generalizations about identity, career path, relationship to family, and behavior in relationships, among others. As Res expressed, "if race didn't really matter, the category wouldn't exist." His pragmatism, maturity, and pride in his multiracial identity can serve as a model as campuses become peopled with students who resemble Res' multicultural self.

Link to Considerations Beyond Oneself

Community

With the alleged "Balkanization" of the college campus (Steele, 1990), community as a source of social glue and unity often gets dismissed in discussions of college life. The respondents in this book, particularly the students, belie this well-reported but dubious assumption about fragmentation. According to the research contained in this text, community is alive and well and living on college campuses. This is true at least in part because these respondents and others like them are dedicated to making their campuses a better place to live and study. They are willing to go so far as to sacrifice personal goals (e.g., transferring to another college) in order to exercise critically important leadership on their campuses. This trend, while admittedly not embodied by all students, is a perspective often buried under the accusations of hedonism and individual self-interest of Generation X.

The respondents in this book can teach student affairs educators that their expectations about students' commitment to their communities and to purposes larger than individual self-interest need not be low. Students will surprise us with their willingness to work toward a community that enriches their own and their fellow students' lives.

Unheard and Unacknowledged Voices

A challenge to qualitative researchers, particularly when their research is focused on a single respondent or site, is "so what?" How can the findings and interpretations of the single case study serve the purposes of a college campus? If we cannot generalize due to lack of random sampling and the controls of quantitative analysis, how are the findings to be used by practitioners?

The voices represented in this book enrich the normative and generalized accounts of traditional student development theory. The wisdom of these voices cannot tell you what *all* students of color, university custodians, resident assistants, suicide survivors, and adult children of alcoholics feel and think. But the meaning expressed in this book can provide the reader with insight and more informed understanding about these topics. The research can spur student affairs educators to ask questions rather than rely on an a priori model or theory. The interpretations invite a deeper and richer understanding of campus life. The authors remind student affairs educators that there is tremendous diversity within and between groups of students, regardless of their defining characteristics. Theory need not stereotype or overly direct but rather inform and guide.

The respondents in this book also remind student affairs educators that wisdom about higher education administration, student development, and university life is represented at all levels of the institution. This perspective provides documentation to support more inclusive decision making and release time for staff to participate in institutional governance. Most importantly, their words remind us that collaboration is a worthy goal in student affairs administration.

Role of Qualitative Research in Student Affairs

Student affairs educators use the techniques of qualitative research (e.g., interviewing, observation, document analysis) in their everyday practice (Manning, 1992; Stage, 1992). Jeni Hart (personal communication, May 8, 1997), a chapter author, shared her thoughts about the influence of qualitative research on her administrative practice.

> The skills learned in naturalistic [constructivist] inquiry influence all educational opportunities I have with students. I use qualitative methods daily to define problems, to look for themes and trends, to make meaning from multiple and diverse perspectives, and to evaluate policies and programs. While data that emerge through an individual conversation may not meet the standards of trustworthiness or authenticity, utilizing qualitative methods helps me to be a better supervisor, judicial officer, and educator. . . . Qualitative research helps me look deeper at a situation.

Student affairs educators consistently sift through the data collected (e.g., student testimony at a disciplinary hearing, feedback during an open forum) to form interpretations and conclusions. These interpretations, richly informative, are extended through administrative action and practice to become policies, programs, and ways of operating. The decisions, based on data and the analysis attendant with the use of those data, become institutionalized into the practices of the profession.

Summary

In keeping with the collaborative and cooperative goals of constructivist inquiry, the following words, offered by Jeni Hart (personal
communication, May 8, 1997), provide insight about the uses of
qualitative research in student affairs practice.

> Qualitative research has reinforced the idea of mattering. I have
> learned through this method of inquiry that each respondent, or in
> my daily interactions, each student, matters and has value. I see it
> as my responsibility as an educator to shape meaning through dia-
> logue with students. Diverse and multiple perspectives only provide
> a more fertile environment in which to work, teach, and learn.

References

Baxter Magolda, M. (1992). *Knowing and reasoning in college:
Gender-related patterns in students' intellectual development.* San Francisco, CA: Jossey-Bass.

Belenky, M., Clinchy, B., Golberger, N., & Tarule, J. (1986). *Wom-
en's ways of knowing: The development of self, voice, and mind.* New
York, NY: Basic Books.

Cross, W., (1991). *Shades of black: Diversity in African-American
identity.* Philadelphia, PA: Temple University Press.

Gilligan, C. (1982). *In a different voice: Psychological theory and
women's development.* Cambridge, MA: Harvard University Press.

Lee, C. C., & Richardson, B. L. (1991). *Multicultural issues in counseling: New approaches to diversity.* Alexandria, VA: American Association for Counseling and Development.

Manning, K. (1989). *Campus rituals and cultural meaning.* Unpublished doctoral dissertation, Indiana University, Bloomington.

Manning, K. (1992). A rationale for using qualitative research in
student affairs. *Journal of College Student Development, 33*(2), 132–136.

McEwen, M., Roper, L., Bryant, D. R., & Langa, M. (1990). Incorporating the development of African-American students into psychosocial theories of student development. *Journal of College Student Development, 31*, 429–436.

Pederson, P. (1988). *Handbook for developing multicultural awareness*. Alexandria, VA: American Association of Counseling and Development.

Stage, F. (1992). *Diverse methods for research and assessment of college students*. Alexandria, VA: American College Personnel Association Media.

Steele, S. (1990). *The content of our character: A new vision for race in America*. New York, NY: St. Martin's Press.

Sue, D.W., & Sue, D. (1990). *Counseling the cultural different: Theory and practice*. Wiley & Sons.

About the Contributors

Kelly Haggerty Ahuna

A 1991 graduate of the University of Vermont's Higher Education and Student Affairs Administration (HESA) program, Kelly Haggerty Ahuna is currently a doctoral student in sociology of education at the State University of New York at Buffalo. Her dissertation research focuses on the gender consciousness of working class and middle class white college women in both traditional and non-traditional fields. She also teaches an undergraduate course in critical thinking.

Jennifer Hart

Jennifer Hart graduated from the University of Vermont's HESA program in 1993. She is currently a doctoral student in the Center for the Study of Higher Education at the University of Arizona. She is enrolled in the Organization and Administration program. Her research interests centered on feminism and professional work in the academy.

Kathleen Manning

Dr. Manning is an associate professor in the HESA graduate program at the University of Vermont where she has taught since 1989. She received her doctorate from Indiana University in Higher Education Administration; a masters in Student Personnel Services at the

State University of New York at Albany; and a bachelor of arts in biology from Marist College. Her research interests include cultural pluralism, anti-racism, qualitative research, and organizational theory in higher education.

Melissa Bronzino Regan

Melissa Bronzino Regan works in career services at her alma mater, Trinity College in Hartford, Connecticut. She created, implemented, and oversees an extensive series of programs involving alumni/ae in Career Services. Prior to joining Career Services in 1996, she was a member of Trinity's development team where she held a number of positions from the annual fund to major gifts. She graduated from the University of Vermont's HESA program in 1990 and now lives in Avon, Connecticut with her husband, Tom and their daughter, Chelsea.

Elizabeth A. Skeffington

Elizabeth Skeffington is the Associate Dean of Student Development at Mount St. Mary's College in Emmitsburg, Maryland. She graduated from the University of Vermont Higher Education and Student Affairs Administration Program in May, 1995.

Timothy Wilson

Tim Wilson is a 1997 graduate of Vermont's HESA program. After graduating from San Diego State University with a B.S. in Marketing in 1992, Tim worked as a Resident Director for two years at Willamette University. He is currently the Coordinator for the Office of Multicultural Affairs at the University of Missouri-Columbia.

Michael Paul A. Wong

Michael Paul A. Wong is a Ph.D. candidate in higher education policy and organization at the University of Southern California and a Resident Director at California State University at Los Angeles. He received his M.Ed from The University of Vermont HESA program in 1992. His current research interests include faculty roles and the service function, critical theory, qualitative methodology, and the role of higher education in the U.S.